CITYSPOTS

TALLINN

Ann Carroll Burgess & Tom Burgess

Thomas Cook

Written by Ann Carroll Burgess & Tom Burgess
Front cover photography courtesy of A1pix

Produced by 183 Books
Design/layout/maps: Chris Lane and Lee Biggadike
Editorial/project management: Stephen York

Published by Thomas Cook Publishing
A division of Thomas Cook Tour Operations Limited
PO Box 227, Units 15/16, Coningsby Road
Peterborough PE3 8SB, United Kingdom
email: books@thomascook.com
www.thomascookpublishing.com
+44 (0) 1733 416477

First edition © 2006 Thomas Cook Publishing
Text © 2006 Thomas Cook Publishing
Maps © 2006 Thomas Cook Publishing
ISBN-13: 978-1-84157-552-0
ISBN-10: 1-84157-552-6
Head of Thomas Cook Publishing: Chris Young
Project Editor: Kelly Anne Pipes
Production/DTP: Steven Collins

Printed and bound in Spain by GraphyCems

CONTENTS

SYMBOLS & ABBREVIATIONS

The following symbols are used throughout this book:

☏ telephone	🖷 fax	✉ email	🌐 website address
ⓐ address	🕔 opening times	Ⓝ public transport connections

The following symbols are used on the maps:

ⓘ Tourist Information Office

✈ Airport

Hotels and restaurants are graded by approximate price as follows:

€ budget price **€€** mid-range price **€€€** expensive

The local currency is the Estonian Kroon (see page 145)

24-HOUR CLOCK

All times in this book are given in the 24-hour clock system used widely in Europe and in most international transport timetables.

⬤ *Church spires, domes, and towers add to Tallinn's enchanting skyline*

Introduction

Imagine a city with a well-preserved medieval town, tasty beer, a lively nightlife and a population well versed in English. You might find yourself surprised to be dreaming of Tallinn.

If you don't fall in love with this lively city instantly, it won't be long before you do. Gothic spires sprout like wildflowers from the Old Town, while new office and apartment towers grow steadily in the city centre.

It would be easy to compare Tallinn to any other older city. To do so would deny the Estonian capital's unique and individual flavour.

With a population of only 400,000, Tallinn is small compared to most European capitals. However, a lot is packed into this small city, and most major points of interest are within 2 km of the centre of town, making feet the preferred mode of transport. Couple this with clean air, clean streets, no traffic congestion, and warm and friendly residents, and you will find it is very easy to walk around Tallinn.

The Old Town section of the city is the major draw for most visitors: a pleasing jumble of 14th- and 15th-century buildings topped with turrets and spires and paved with cobblestones. You could lay out a plan to diligently conquer this area or simply roam its narrow streets filled with cafes, shops, churches and museums.

The best deal in town is a Tallinn Card (available for 6, 24, 48 or 72 hours, ranging in price from 130–450Kr./€8–25), which, for one reasonable price, gives you access to most museums, attractions, public transport and discounts on other entertainment.

Tallinn, of all the Baltic cities, is the most visitor-friendly. Don't forget to look up Fat Margaret and Tall Herman while you are there.

● *It's not just church roofs that look attractive in the Old Town*

When to go

SEASONS & CLIMATE

Tallinn's climate is controlled by incoming streams of warm water from the Atlantic Ocean, moderated by the Baltic Sea. This gives Tallinn a moderate, maritime climate, with summers not too hot, and winters not too cold. The humidity in summer can be high, up to 80 per cent. Thus, Tallinn tends to be rather cloudy and damp, with an average of about 500 mm (19.5 in) of precipitation a year.

Spring starts in mid-April, and comes in quickly, with an explosion of green in the fields, and multicoloured flowers everywhere. May through September is the best time to visit. July and August, although the warmest months, are also the wettest, with frequent showers. Mid-summer temperatures average 16°C (60°F) and can reach more than 30°C (86°F). May, June and September are the most comfortable. Autumn is long and warm.

Winter gets serious in November, and lasts until April, with snow usually on the ground from late December until late March. Winter temperatures average -5°C (23°F) and rarely go over 4°C (39°F).

April and October tend to be unpredictable, with both cold wintry days, and warm spring-like days.

Due to the city's cultural attractions, visiting at any time of year can be rewarding. During Advent there is a Christmas Market at Raekoja plats, selling treats, gingerbread and handicrafts.

ANNUAL EVENTS

The summer solstice, the longest day of the year, reigns supreme as the holiday that most Estonians look forward to with immense

● *There's more than a chance of snow if you visit early in the year*

pleasure. The entire country takes time off to revel in the long, long day of sunshine with beer drinking, picnicking in the country, folk dancing and music.

The long summer days are enthusiastically celebrated with all kinds of music and dance festivals embracing not only Estonian culture but also those from around the world. It's time for medieval markets, beer fests and some good ol' rock'n'roll nights.

Late autumn and winter don't mean a slowdown in activity for the city. Film festivals, concerts and dances simply move the fun indoors.

And in December the Tallinn Christmas Market returns to Town Hall Square. A gigantic Christmas tree is the centrepiece of the fair, surrounded by huts selling everything from handicrafts to food. Live performers entertain, and, of course, there is always a visit from Santa.

January
Open Music Festival A month-long festival of concerts held in the historical venues of Old Town Tallinn. ⓐ Eesti Kontsert. ⓣ 614 7700. ⓦ www.concert.ee

April
Estonian Music Days This festival is devoted to new music based on classical Estonian works. Held since 1979. ⓐ Estonian Composers Union. ⓣ 645 4068, 646 6536. ⓦ www.ehl.kul.ee

St George's Day Fair at Vanaturu Square Handicrafts and farm goods are for sale, plus brooms and brushes to get you ready for Walpurgis Night at the end of the month when witches take to the skies. ⓐ Estonian Folk Art and Craft Union. ⓣ 660 4772. ⓦ www.folkart.ee

Jazzkaar One of Tallinn's best-attended festivals is this international jazz festival, incorporating traditional with cutting-edge music. Held in venues in Tallinn and around the countryside. Jazzkaar Friends Society also organise other jazz events throughout the year.
📞 611 4405. 🌐 www.jazzkaar.ee

June

Old Town Days Every year for four days in the summer, the Town Hall Square is turned into a Medieval Market overflowing with goods, handicrafts and art. Scattered within the confines of the old city you'll find tradesmen plying their trades and noble citizens, jesters and musicians wandering the streets. Join in the fun and bargain

PUBLIC HOLIDAYS

These dates show public holidays in 2006. Tallinn celebrates both independence and the regaining of it from the Soviets.
New Year's Day 1 Jan
Independence Day 24 Feb
Good Friday 14 Apr
Easter Sunday 16 Apr
Spring Day 1 May
Whitsunday 4 June
Victory Day 23 June
St John's Day 24 June
Day of Restoration of Independence 20 Aug
Christmas Eve 24 Dec
Christmas Day 25 Dec
Second Day of Christmas 26 Dec

with the merchants, listen to the musicians and taste the days of old. ☎ 645 7220. ⓦ www.vip.ee

Celebration of St John's Day Bonfires, dancing, music, games and legends are all a part of the mid-summer festival celebrating the longest day of the year. ⓐ Estonian Open Air Museum (see page 86). ☎ 654 9100. ⓦ www.evm.ee

July

Beer Summer The biggest beer fest in the Baltics comes to Tallinn every summer. Held over five days at the Song Festival Grounds where you can drink beer, hear rock, reggae, blues, jazz and Estonian music. ⓐ Meediaekspress. ☎ 611 2112. ⓦ www.ollesummer.ee

Medieval Market in the Old Town Ancient trade folk bring their skills to life while musicians, nobles and fools roam the streets in period costume. Estonian Folk Art And Craft Union: ☎ 660 4772. ⓦ www.folkart.ee

August

August Dancefestival A lively international festival of dancing, highlighting emerging new artists. Events are held mainly at Kanuti Gildi Saal. ⓐ Pikk 20 ☎ 646 4704. ⓦ www.saal.ee

October

International New Music Festival A festival of contemporary music composed inside and outside the borders of Estonia. An average of more than a hundred new works are introduced at the concerts. Held every two years, the next time will be in 2007. ⓦ www.concert.ee

November
Tallinn Black Night Film Festival This film festival is unique in combining feature-length films with sub-festivals of animated films and works from students. Pimedate Ööde Filmifestival: ☎ 628 4510. Ⓦ www.poff.ee

December
Christmas Market Town hall square in Old Town comes alive with the sights and sounds of Christmas every day until 26 December. A huge Christmas tree is the showpiece, surrounded by a multitude of huts selling crafts, food, ornaments and toys. ⓐ Ober-House Schlössle. ☎ 679 8585.

Christmas Jazz Music to lighten the darkest nights begins in late November and continues through December. Participating artists from around the world have included Charles Lloyd, Omar Sosa and Von Krahl. For tickets and schedule Ⓦ www.jazzkaar.ee

🔻 *Getting medieval in Tallinn for the Old Town Days*

The Spa Experience

The spa experience in Tallinn (and in the Baltics generally) differs greatly from North American and western European spas which focus primarily on physical fitness and physical beauty. The major intent of spas in this area is to improve your health – to address muscle aches, and problems such as high blood cholesterol and diabetes.

Of course, you will find that at the major establishments there are plenty of fitness and beauty programmes to complement the health components.

What are the best reasons to visit a spa in Tallinn? The price. The services. And the destination. Most of the spas in Tallinn – and throughout Estonia – are set along beach areas, and even if you don't want to partake of the spa programme you'll find these establishments offer very reasonably priced hotel accommodation.

You may discover that some unusual charges such as for a bathrobe, a refrigerator in the room or bicycle rentals are not included in the main price.

And, as with all spas, be sure to arrive for your appointments 15–20 minutes early to allow time to be assigned a locker, take a warming shower if necessary, and dress appropriately for the desired activity.

SPAS IN TALLINN

Pirita TOP Spa Hotel A top-notch hotel right at the mouth of the Pirita River and close to the beaches. The spa has programmes for both health and beauty.

Spa services include body massage, herbal and pearl baths,

electrotherapy, paraffin treatments, inhalation therapy, stretching, curative gymnastics and water gymnastics. There is also a full range of exfoliation and traditional beauty treatments. ❷ Regati pst. 1. ❶ 639 8600. ❶ 639 8821. Ⓦ www.topspa.ee

Viimsi Tervis Spa Hotel Located on the Viimsi peninsula minutes from Tallinn's city centre. A modern hotel with more than 100 rooms, all equipped with hair dryer, TV, radio and telephone. All rooms are allergen free.

Spa services include classical massage and massage with hot stones, cellulite treatments, body wrapping, facials, manicures and pedicures. ❷ Randvere tee 11. ❶ 606 1000. ❶ 606 1010. Ⓦ www.viimsitervis.ee

▼ Many hotels have areas devoted to health and fitness

History

Due to its strategic location between Eastern and Western Europe,
Tallinn has a long and varied history, marked by many changes and
foreign influences.

The area around Tallinn was first settled about 3500 years ago by
Finno-Ugric people migrating north. The settlement slowly grew,
and by the 10th century it was an important trading city for
Scandinavian and Russian merchants. By the middle of the 12th
century, Tallinn was shown on world maps.

In the 13th century, German 'Knights of the Sword' arrived, bringing
Christianity and Western European culture and economics to Tallinn. In
1219, Tallinn was conquered by the Danes under King Waldemar II.
Tallinn acquired its current name during this period, the name being
derived from *Taani linn* (Danish city). During the Danish period
(1219–1346) *Toompea* (Dome hill) was developed – including the
construction of the Dome Cathedral – and so was the layout of the
street network that still exists today. In 1285, Tallinn joined the
Hanseatic League, and gained economically as a trading city.

In 1346, Denmark sold Northern Estonia, including Tallinn, to
Germany. For the next two hundred years, known as the 'Golden
Age', Tallinn flourished due to its important strategic location
between Western Europe and Russia. Tallinn grew into one of the
biggest and most powerful towns in Northern Europe, fortified with
66 defensive towers.

The Lutheran Reformation of 1524 replaced the Catholic Church
with the Lutheran Church, which began school education for the
citizens. The Livonian War, a three-party affair between Russia,
Poland and Sweden, with Estonia caught in the middle, ended the
Golden Age and, in 1561, the Swedes captured Tallinn, although it

took another 65 years before all of Estonia fell under Swedish rule.

Although referred to as 'The Good Old Swedish Times', Tallinn languished economically for 150 years. However, during this period there was rapid development of school education for Estonians.

Tallinn was captured by the Russians in the Northern War in 1710. The Tsars allowed Tallinn a fair amount of autonomy, and started building the city into an important Russian port, as well as developing it as an industrial city.

After World War I and the Russian Revolution, Estonia declared itself independent on 24 February 1918, but it took two years of fighting against both Germany and Russia before Estonia's independence was recognised by the Tartu Peace Treaty on 2 February 1920.

Under independence, Tallinn again flourished, both economically and culturally. This ended with World War II, with first Russia, then Germany, and finally Russia once more occupying Estonia. Tallinn languished behind the Iron Curtain.

With the fall of Soviet Russia, Estonia once again declared independence on 20 August 1991. Under independence, Tallinn is once again thriving and is quickly developing into a modern and open city. Estonia joined the European Union on 1 May 2004.

Tallinn's citizens are now free to celebrate their culture however they like

Lifestyle

What a difference a decade makes! Such a short time ago you would find people having to queue for such necessities as toothpaste and tomatoes. Now there are major department stores and malls, expensive cars parked on cobblestoned streets and a population that appears happy to welcome a flood of tourists. Tourists will find costs to be very reasonable, Estonia is not as expensive to visit as Sweden or as cheap as Slovakia, just nicely affordable.

Estonians are typically a somewhat shy people until they get to know you. Then you will discover that they can be quite fun-loving and outgoing. The café and bar scene is a huge part of everyday Estonian life. Expect thought-provoking dialogues from well-educated locals in the cafés during the day and lively party scenes in the clubs and pubs at night. Tallinn seems to hold more and longer festivals than any other country in the Baltics.

As traditional, conservative and quiet as the Estonians may be, their secret side is very high-tech. Estonians use the internet more than any other country in the world. Technology aside, if you ask an Estonian his or her idea of bliss the reply might well be 'a walk in the woods' or 'a day spent fishing'. For all their urban lifestyle and wi-fi technology Estonians are at heart naturalists.

BE A GOOD GUEST

When entering someone's home always remove your shoes. And don't forget to bring some flowers for your host.

● *Alfresco cafés have sprung up all around the city*

Culture

Tallinn cannot rival metropolis like London or New York in size and international standing, but that doesn't mean it lacks for cultural activities, or that all require a costume. Tallinn's true wealth lies in the nature of its people. They are avid theatre and concert attendees, as well as devout readers.

Music is a major part of Estonian life and both the National Symphony Orchestra and National Opera have earned solid reputations worldwide. Aside from the traditional concert hall venues of the Great and Small Guilds, the Old City has a plethora of atmospheric sites for music that include medieval churches.

Did we say that Estonians are avid readers? You bet they are. On an average day an Estonian will read at least 3 or 4 newspapers and devour an enormous number of books each year. The Tallinn Central Library opened in 1907 and is one of the oldest in Estonia. For a city of less than a half million people to have a main library and some 22 branches notes a city of true bibliophiles.

Live theatre is another favorite pastime of Tallinn residents. From the traditional Estonian Drama Theatre to the cutting-edge presentations of the Salon Theatre and Theatre NO99, Estonians appear to embrace theatre in all its forms. Even youngsters are introduced to live theatre at the Estonian Puppet Theatre and the Trumm Children's Theatre troupe. A truly avant-garde experience is the Von Krahl Theatre that performs in a cabaret-like hall.

Music is more than just a part of the Estonian culture. More than any other element, music is the frame that holds the tapestry of culture in this country. The tradition of folk music is centuries old and Estonia boasts of one of the largest collections of folk songs in the world, with written records of about 133,000 songs. It is no wonder that their break from the Soviet came with the 'Singing Revolution'. Music is such a part of the cultural life in the city that you can hear some kind of performance almost every night.

Since Estonia regained its independence with the fall of the Soviet Union, cultural life has begun a rapid evolution embracing all kinds of new media and virtual art. Yet, it continues to hold dear its traditions. Every four years the Quadrennial Song and Dance Festival takes place in Tallinn, beginning with a festive parade of performers to the Song Festival Grounds located in the suburb of Pirita.

Live theatre, opera, symphony, folk music, choirs, art, newspapers, magazines and, of course, the dialogues in the coffee houses are all parts of Estonia's complex, lively, and ever-evolving cultural scene.

The Song Festival Grounds celebrate a part of the fabric of Estonian life

THE SINGING REVOLUTION

Song festivals have played a strong role in Baltic life since the nineteenth century, when the rediscovery of folk songs started to rejuvenate the indigenous cultures weakened by centuries of foreign domination. During the Soviet period, song festivals were the only expression of national solidarity that were tolerated by the occupiers.

In 1988, the labour unions and the Estonian Heritage Society organized a massive Song Festival at the Song Festival Grounds in Tallinn (see page 21). The festival became the focus of mass demonstrations against the occupation by the Soviet regime. This movement became known as the 'Singing Revolution', and the term was used to describe the independence movement in all three Baltic States – Estonia, Latvia and Lithuania.

Perhaps the greatest demonstration of inter-Baltic solidarity occurred on 23 August 1989, when some two million people joined hands to form a human chain stretching from Tallinn to Vilnius.

In 1991, the 'singers' were freed, but the song festivals continue, and the sound of thousands of performers singing in unison is emotionally very powerful.

● *The colourful clockface of the Church of the Holy Ghost*

Shopping

If you last visited Tallinn when the Soviets were in charge, you are in for a bit of a surprise. The shopping scene has changed exponentially. Tallinn hasn't just embraced capitalism – it's engaged in a raving love affair.

Amber, amber and more amber. You'll find more places to buy this Baltic treasure than you could have possibly imagined. But *caveat emptor*! Telling the real from the fake requires at least a match – plastic melts, amber doesn't.

Tallinn doesn't lack for any number of places to spend your money. The Old Town is filled with dozens of souvenir, antique, clothing and speciality shops. The most popular souvenir items are knitted goods like sweaters and mittens, patchwork quilts, trinkets proclaiming the city name, and spirits. The main shopping streets in the Old Town are Viru, Muurivahe, Suur-Karja, plus Kullassepa near Town Hall Square.

You'll find some craftsmen in the Old Town plying their wares along Muurivahe. The prices are cheaper but you'll probably need to shake the dust off any item you buy.

At the other end of the retailing scale, you'll find young women squeezed into T-shirts hawking postcards outside nearly every tourist attraction. A flea market near the Old Town can turn up such lovely finds as a pure linen poncho or leather goods, and if you can't live without a Russian-made fur hat this is also a good place to look. Try out your bargaining skills, but not too aggressively.

Stockmann (see page 84) and Kaubamaja, the two largest department stores in town, stock everything you could desire, from clothing and cosmetics to electronics. These locations are your best bet for any item you left at home.

Don't overlook the shopping centres, which can be glitzy, airy malls. The newest is Viru Keskus in Viru Square, which contains the largest bookshop in the Baltics, an art gallery and the usual stores. The Kristine Centre is, unsurprisingly, located in Kristine, and has clothing, grocery and speciality stores all in one place.

For upmarket chic in the Old Town, try the smaller Demini Centre (ⓐ Viru 1) which is another good place to purchase handicrafts to take home.

AMBER

Valued as an ornament since ancient times, amber is still important in the Baltic today, with souvenir shops offering amber in all shapes and sizes. Amber is the fossilised resin of pines trees that existed some 50 million years ago. Although mostly deposited on the westerns side of the Baltic, due to tidal currents much amber is washed ashore in the eastern Baltic states of Estonia, Latvia and Lithuania.

It is traditionally 'mined' simply by beachcombing – you can see people combing the beaches for amber nuggets, especially after a storm. Amber is usually a clear translucent nugget. Normally orange-brown in colour, although many other colours exist, this probably due to the presence of other minerals that were absorbed as the resin was hardening.

If purchasing amber, be sure to make sure it is authentic, as many imitations made of glass, plastic and copal (hardened resin from modern trees) exist. One way to test for amber is to touch it with a hot wire or hot needle point. If it has an acrid resinous smell, it is probably amber. If it has a sweet resinous smell, a plastic smell, or no smell, then it is probably fake.

Opening hours for most shops are generally 10.00–19.00, closing earlier on Saturdays and remaining closed on Sundays. Some exceptions may be found in the tourist areas of the Old Town.

USEFUL SHOPPING PHRASES

What time do the shops open/close?
Mis kell kauplused avatakse/suletakse?
Mis kell kah-up-lused ahvah-tahkse/su-letahk-se?

How much is this?
Kui palju see maksab?
Kuy pal-yu se-eh mak-sab?

Can I try this on?
Kas ma tohin seda proovida?
Kas mah toh-hin seh-da pro-o-vi-da?

My size is ...
Minu number on ...
Mi-nuh nub-ber on ...

I'll take this one, thank you
Aitäh, ma võtan selle
Ay-tahh, mah vo-tan sel-leh

Can you show me the one in the window/this one?
Näidake mulle palun seda vaateaknalt/seda?
Nay-da-keh mul-leh pah-loon seh-da vah-ah-te-ahk-nalt/seh-da?

This is too large/too small/too expensive
See on liiga suur/liiga väike/liiga kallis.
Se-eh on lee-ga su-ur/lee-ga vay-keh/lee-ga kal-lis.

◀ *Medieval fairs are a marketplace for traditional crafts and foodstuffs*

Eating & drinking

Estonian cuisine is an adventure in cholesterol. The national cuisine is rich in meat, potatoes and dairy products, with pork, cheese and sour cream involved in some manner with almost every dish. Rye bread, salted herring and beer are also traditional foods.

A traditional Estonian starter is *sult*, a mixture of pork pieces set in jelly. It is an acquired taste. Most restaurants feature salted herring, smoked eel and sliced sausage, all served with delicious dark rye bread, as a starter.

Soup can be either a starter or a snack for lunch. The most common soup is *seljanka*, a Russian broth of meat, pickled vegetables and fish. Other light meals include *pelminid* (akin to Italian ravioli), *pirukas* (dough stuffed with bacon and cabbage), and pancakes with cheese, meat or mushrooms. Salads are becoming more common. You may want to try a traditional Estonian salad of peas and pickles served in sour cream. Plates of greens, often laced with tuna, are also a local favourite.

The standard Estonian main course is pork with potatoes and sauerkraut. The pork comes either as roast, or as a chop in batter. It usually has a good rind of fat which, when properly cooked, is quite delicious. Other meat courses, based on beef, chicken and

PRICE RATING

The restaurant price guides used in the book indicate the approximate cost of a three-course meal for one person, excluding drinks, at the time of writing.

€ up to €20   **€€** €20–30   **€€€** more than €30

⬩ *Cafés and bars in Tallinn range from traditional to the trendy*

blood sausage, are common, as are pan-fried freshwater fish such as trout, perch and pike.

Vegetarians shouldn't despair about visiting Tallinn, although the options may be somewhat limited. Try Gauranga (ⓐ Gonsori 12. ⓦ www.gauranga.ee), which promises to be '108 per cent vegetarian'. The best bet is to head to other ethnic eateries.

As Tallinn becomes more cosmopolitan, a much wider variety of ethnic foods from around the world is becoming available, with French, Italian, Greek, Indian, Japanese and Chinese restaurants, just to mention a few, already well established.

Estonians love their sweets. The most common dessert is

mannapuder (semolina pudding), often served with fruits and berries. Pancakes filled with jam are another local favourite. Cakes, flans, tortes and cheesecake are widely available.

On the liquid side, the Estonians prefer coffee or soft drinks in the daytime, and beer, beer, beer in the evening. Estonians frequent coffee shops during the day, and they normally take it black. If you want cream or sugar, you will have to ask for it. Espresso or cappuccino are available, but filter coffee is most common. The coffee is usually accompanied by a sticky bun or small piece of cake.

There are an increasing number of bars and pubs in Tallinn, most in the English and American style. The beer normally comes as a regular lager and the locals consume a lot of it. Stronger beers and ales are also available. Beer is normally sold by the half litre, and ordering lesser amounts is frowned upon. A traditional Estonian spirit is *Vana Tallinn*. A rather syrupy and medicinal liqueur, it is easier to take watered down with fruit juice or coffee. Thanks to the Russian influence, good vodka is also readily available, and at good prices.

Restoran, meaning restaurant, indicates a more upmarket establishment, complete with menus and table service. There are many of these in Tallinn, including in most major hotels. For something more informal, try a café, where you order and pay at the counter. Many pubs and bars also offer a full menu.

For a medieval dining experience, try the Olde Hansa Restoran, in the Old Town, where the menu is taken from the late 15th century. ⓐ Vana Turg 1. ⓣ 627 9020. ⓦ www.oldehansa.ee.

With Tallinn's abundance of green spaces and parks, especially adjacent to the Old Town, you should take a 'picnic in the park' one sunny afternoon. Supermarkets can supply you with the basics of bread, cheese, meats and soft drinks, while bakeries can supply bread and pastries.

USEFUL DINING PHRASES

I would like a table for ... people
Ma soovin lauda ... inimesele
Mah so-ov-in lau-da ...ih-ni-meh-seh-leh

Waiter/waitress!
Kelner! Ettekandja!
Kelner! Ettekandyah!

May I have the bill, please?
Ma palun arve?
Mah pah-loon ar-veh?

Could I have it well-cooked/medium/rare please?
Palun praadige liha tugevalt/keskmiselt/pooltooreks?
Pah-loon pra-a-di-ghe ly-hah tuh-ghe-valt/kesk-mi-selt/ poh-ohl-toh-oh-reks?

I am a vegetarian. Does this contain meat?
Ma olen taimetoitlane. Kas see sisaldab liha?
Ma olen tayme-toytlane. Kahs se-eh see-sahl-dahb liha?

Where is the toilet (restroom) please?
Palun, kus asub WC?
Pah-loon, kus a-sup veh-tseh?

I would like a cup of/two cups of/another coffee/tea
Ma palun ühe tassi/kaks tassi/veel kohvi/teed
Mah pah-loon yu-heh tas-si/kaks tas-si/ve-el koh-vi/te-ed

I would like a beer/two beers, please
Palun üks õlu/kaks õlut
Pah-loon yuks oh-lyuh/kaks oh-lyuht

Entertainment & nightlife

Don't be surprised that a small city can have quite a variety of night-life and after-hours entertainment available. Tallinn seems capable of accommodating almost every taste from the ear-splitting rock of a packed nightclub to the quiet sophistication of cigar and brandy lounge.

You'll find most of the night scene in and around Tallinn's Old Town. You won't need to make plans to visit a specific club; simply wander from place to place until you find one that suits your style. Some are just metres apart from each other.

Timing is everything. Friday night is the night to party in Tallinn. The party reaches fever pitch between 23.00–03.00. Thursdays and Saturdays are also quite lively, but the rest of the week can be almost dull by comparison to Friday. During the week the bars are usually open only until midnight and some clubs don't even bother to open on a Sunday, Monday or Tuesday.

The bar scene not quite your style? Tallinn's cultural life outside the bar is wide and varied. The National Symphony and National Opera are two stalwarts that can be counted on for quality performances. You'll also discover that the small venues of the Old Town include churches that offer medieval and Early Music performances. Chamber music concerts are frequently held in the House of Blackheads.

Theatre is not to be overlooked in the city, although most of the performances will be in Estonian. If you can spend an evening enthralled in stage craft you'll not want to miss the chance of attending a play or two.

● *Tallinn has a very vibrant club scene*

A live performance of music will transcend any language barriers and Tallinn boasts no shortage of concerts and performances. Yes, you'll find lots of classical and operatic music but Tallinn is heavily into jazz, pop, and all kinds of contemporary sounds.

Need your entertainment on a big screen? Tallinn is home to the Dark Nights Film Festival, held in December. During the rest of the year you'll find many multi-plex theatres showing both mainstream and art films, many in English with Estonian subtitles. The Kosmos features mostly Hollywood fare, try the Soprus or Kinomaja for more avant-garde selections.

Sport & relaxation

SPECTATOR SPORTS

Basketball and football are the two biggest spectator sports in Estonia, although Estonians are not really big on either, probably due to the lack of success by national teams in international competition. This may change, as the national football team recently defeated the Russians in an exhibition match.

Basketball, hockey and other sports are held in the Saku Arena, which is also a venue for concerts (see page 84). ❸ Paldiski maantee 104b. ❶660 0216. Ⓦ www.sakuarena.com. Football matches are held at A. Le Coq Arena. ❸ Lillekula Stadium. Asula 4c.

Horse racing, especially trotting with sulkies (two-wheeled carts), is popular in Tallinn. Racing takes place at the Tallinn hippodrome. ❸ Paldiski maantee 5. ❶ 677 1677. Ⓦ www.hipodroom.ee. A current sports hero is Marko Martin, one of the world's top rally drivers. Many Estonians follow him to the World Rally Championship events in other parts of Europe. Olympic heroes include Erki Nool, who won a gold medal in the Decathlon in 2000.

WINTER SPORTS

With the long winters, skiing is popular in Estonia. The best skiing is cross-country, as there are few hills high enough for a good downhill run. Otepaa, in southern Estonia, is the leading ski resort. Estonian cross-country skier Andrus Veerpalu won gold and silver medals at the 2002 Winter Olympics.

PARTICIPATION & RELAXATION

In the summer months, Estonians take to the great outdoors, with hiking, canoeing, cycling and birdwatching popular activities. Most of this is done well outside Tallinn in places such as Lahemaa National Park, Soomaa National Park, or along the many kilometres of Baltic coastline. These areas have well-maintained hiking trails and nature paths. Deer, moose and elk are commonly sighted along these trails, as are the occasional bear and wild boar.

Exercise and fitness are big in Estonia. Some major hotels offer exercise facilities and swimming pools. If you want to jog, stick to Pirita and Kadriorg, as other areas of the city are dimly lit, and have many dogs on the loose. Tallinn has several clubs that offer aerobics, weightlifting and yoga, and many have swimming pools and saunas.

Facilities for basketball, billiards, bowling, cycling, horse riding, ice skating, swimming, skating, squash and tennis are also available in the city – the tourist office can provide details.

⬤ *High-tech gamblers bet on sulky racing online, as well as at the hippodrome*

Accommodation

As the economy continues to grow so do the hotels. New hotels are springing up like daisies to accommodate the ever-growing tourist demand. As a rule of thumb the most luxurious establishments are located in the Old Town area, with more economical choices found in the city centre and in the suburbs. Most of the budget hotels are products of the Soviet era and are not likely to have been renovated. However, you will find that many budget hotels and hostels are just a short tram or bus ride away from the action of the Old Town.

HOSTELS

Academic Hostel € Located in the grounds of the Tallinn Technical University, this hostel offers brand-new rooms for one or two people, shared baths, kitchen, dining room, laundry facilities and internet connection. ⓐ Akadeemia tee 11. ❶ 620 2275. ❶ 620 2276. ⓦ www.academichostel.com

Eurohostel € Near Town Hall Square, an excellent Old Town choice for backpackers and budget travellers. The interiors are simple and there are both double rooms and dorms that sleep 4 to 6. ⓐ Nunne 2. ❶/❶ 644 7788. ⓦ www.eurohostel.com

Estonian Youth Hostel Association ⓐ Tatari 39. ❶ 646 1595. ⓔ puhkemajad@online.ee

HOTELS

Comfort Hotel Oru €–€€ New but cosy hotel conveniently located for attractions in Kadriorg and Pirita. ⓐ Narva 120B. ❶ 603 3302. ❶ 601 2600. ⓦ www.oruhotel.ee

Hotel G9 €€ Located on the third floor of a Stalinist-era office building, this is a simple hotel with very basic services. However, the price is right and the city-centre location is good. ⓐ Gonsiori 9. ① 626 7100. ① 626 7102. ⓦ www.hotelg9.ee

Meriton Old Town Hotel €€ A nice tourist-class hotel on the edge of the Old Town. The rooms are somewhat small but cheerful in decor. The lobby contains part of the old city wall and the round outer edge of the neighbouring 15th-century mill. ⓐ Lai 49. ① 614 1300.

Domina City €€–€€€ An elegant hotel tucked into the Old Town. The influence is clearly Italian with light marble floors and sweeping staircases. ⓐ Vana-Posti 11/13. ① 681 3900. ① 681 3901. ⓦ www.dominahotels.com

Ecoland €€–€€€ A well-appointed hotel in Pirita, a quiet, forested area at the edge of the city. The decor in the bedrooms can only be described as eclectic, and the price includes a daily sauna. For a truly private experience rent one of the garden bungalows. ⓐ Randvere tee 115. ① 605 1999. ① 605 1998. ⓦ www.ecoland.ee

Romeo Family Hotel €€–€€€ The only family-run hotel in the Old Town offers a level of personal service that's hard to beat. Each of

PRICE RATING
The ratings below indicate the approximate cost of a room for two people for one night.
€ Under €35. **€€** €36–60. **€€€** €60–120. **€€€+** Over €120.

the spacious rooms of this restored 19th-century building has its own shower and wc. The breakfast area, like the rooms, has a nice cosy atmosphere. ⓐ Suur-Karja 18, 4th floor, Apt. 38. ❶ 644 4255.

Stroomi €€–€€€ Best bet for beach access, this Soviet influenced building is literally 250 m (280 yards) from the beach. A bargain-priced hotel only a 10-min drive west of the city centre. Rents out bicycles and roller skates as well. ⓐ Randla 11. ❶ 630 4200. ❶ 630 4500. ⓦ www.stroomi.ee

Uniquestay €€–€€€ Modern, spartanly furnished and yet warm at the same time. This well-planned city-centre hotel has the connected traveller in mind; each room includes a computer. The cosy café/restaurant in the basement is worth visiting even if you don't stay in the hotel. ⓐ Paldiski mnt 3. ❶ 660 0700. ❶ 661 6176. ⓦ www.uniquestay.com

Baltic Hotel Vana Wiru €€€ Spacious rooms with satellite TV, marbled floors and WiFi in the lobby. This Old Town hotel is living proof that traditional can seamlessly blend with techno. ⓐ Viru 11. ❶ 669 1500. ❶ 669 1501. ⓦ www.vanawiru.ee

Villa Hortensia €€€ This guest house in a recently renovated Old Town Master's Courtyard is an unusual find. The hotel shares its location with a gallery and artisans' workshops, which attracts an artistic clientele. As there is no reception at the guesthouse, you need to phone ahead for the keys. ⓐ Vene 6. ❶ 504 6113.

● *Reputedly the tallest building in Estonia – the Radisson hotel*

Old Town Maestro's €€€ A boutique hotel with art deco influenced interiors and spacious rooms. This six-storey hotel is located in the very heart of the Old Town's night scene. ❸ Suur-Karja 10. ❶ 626 2000. ❶ 631 3333. ⓦ www.maestrohotel.ee

Reval Express Hotel €€€ Modern, efficient hotel – part of a small chain working towards environmental friendliness. Within easy reach of both the Old Town and the ferry terminal. ❸ Sadama 1. ❶ 667 8700. ❶ 667 8800. ⓦ www.revalhotels.com

Scandic Palace €€€ Part of the Hilton International chain, so expect a good, if uninspired, room. The location, however, is terrific, right on the edge of the old city. ❸ Vabaduse väljak 3. ❶ 640 7300. ❶ 640 7299. ⓦ www.scandic-hotels.ee

Scandic St Barbara €€€ This hotel doesn't boast much in the way of frills but the rooms are comfortable and the location is terrific, on the edge of the Old Town. If you must stay connected you'll find a computer in the lobby for guest use. ❸ Roosikrantsi 2A. ❶ 640 7600. ❶ 640 7430. ⓦ www.scandic-hotels.ee

L'Ermitage €€€–€€€+ Small and traditional, this is a wonderful place to hide away. The rooms have lots of creature comforts such as internet connections, flatscreen TVs and mini-bars. To top it off it's clean, efficient and downright friendly. Centrally located in the Old Town just west of Toompea Hill. ❸ Toompuiestee 19. ❶ 699 6400. ❶ 699 6401. ⓦ www.lermitagehotel.ee

Radisson SAS Hotel Tallinn €€€–€€€+ You shouldn't have any difficulties what is said to be the tallest building in the country. A business hotel by nature, with health club and sauna. The location is good for both Old Town and the City Centre, and the views from the roof-top bar are stunning. Children under 17 stay for free. ⓐ Rävala 3. ⓣ 682 3500. Ⓦ www.radissonsas.com

Kolm Ode (3 Sisters) €€€+ An outstanding hotel located inside three of the best-known medieval buildings in Estonia. Known locally as The Three Sisters, the buildings look as though they have stepped straight out of a fairy-tale. Inside, this boutique hotel offers comfort in very stylish, individually designed rooms ⓐ Pikk 71. ⓣ 630 6300. ⓕ 630 6301. Ⓦ www.threesistershotel.com

Schlossle €€€+ Truly, a medieval setting. Heavy wooden beams, massive stone fireplaces and wrought-iron chandeliers are just a few of the touches that give this small hotel its baronial ambience. The hotel has been painstakingly renovated right down to the door knobs. If the view doesn't sweep you off your feet the price might. Did you expect a fairy-tale setting would be cheap? ⓐ Pühavaimu 13 Tallinn. ⓣ 699 7700. ⓕ 699 7777. Ⓦ www.schlossle-hotels.com

⬇ *Medieval ambience in the fairy-tale setting of the Old Town*

THE BEST OF TALLINN

TOP 10 ATTRACTIONS

- **Toompea Castle** Sitting at the very top of Toompea hill, Toompea Castle stands as a sentry that for most of Tallinn's history has guarded the city. It is dominated by three defensive towers, the tallest of which, 'Tall Herman', dates from 1371, and proudly flies the Estonian flag (see page 68).

- **St Nicholas's Church** Started in the 13th century, and rebuilt in the 15th century, this imposing church is now a museum holding Tallinn's collection of medieval art (see page 72).

- **Kadriorg** This beautiful park, with a palace in the centre, was built by Tsar Peter the Great for his mistress-cum-Empress, Catherine. The palace now houses the Museum of Foreign Art, and features many impressive pieces (see page 88).

- **Town Hall and Town Hall Square** Raekoja plats (Town Hall Square) is as old as Tallinn itself. Surrounded by medieval buildings painted in pastel colours, the square is a popular rallying point for Estonian patriotism (see page 64).

- **Alexander Nevsky Cathedral** Built in 1900, this relative newcomer does not quite fit architecturally into the rest of Medieval Old Town. A typical onion-domed Russian

🔽 *Find a good vantage point for an aerial view of the city*

Orthodox Church, it sits next to Toompea Castle and can be seen from most parts of the city (see page 66).

- **Great Sea Gate** At the very northern end of the Old Town, the Great Sea Gate is a 16th-century arch flanked by two towers. The larger of the two towers is 'Fat Margaret' (see page 71) .

- **House of the Blackheads** The Brotherhood of the Blackheads was a merchant's guild founded in 1343, and the house was built to house visiting merchants. The house is elaborately decorated in Renaissance style, both inside and out. You can see the inside if you attend one of the regularly scheduled chamber concerts (see page 70).

- **Botanical Gardens** Located in Pirita, the gardens feature a large area dedicated to virtually every type of tree and plant found in Estonia, and then some (see page 92).

- **Open-air Ethnographic Museum** Located on the western outskirts of Tallinn, this brings together over 100 buildings of the 18th and 19th century from around Estonia (see page 94).

- **Church of the Holy Ghost** Built in the 1360s, it is the only church in Tallinn whose exterior remains in its original form. Although simple and humble on the outside, the inside is richly decorated, and contains precious works of medieval art (see page 68).

Your guide to seeing the best that Tallinn has to offer, depending on how much time you have.

HALF-DAY: TALLINN IN A HURRY

If your time for sightseeing is limited to only a few hours, you are in luck. Tallinn is quite compact, with many of the city's top attractions bunched quite close together. So, put on your hiking shoes and let's go. There is no logical way to wander the streets, so use the Town Hall Square as a hub and take side trips out and back.

First, explore the Town Hall Square or Raekoja plats. There are two buildings of interest, the Town Hall to the south, and the Town Council Pharmacy to the north. Behind the Town Hall is the Museum of Photography. There are also lots of coffee shops and souvenir stands here. Just a few steps south of the square is the Tourist Office. Pick up a map of the city here.

The first excursion will be to Toompea. This is the toughest part of the trip, as it features a steep climb. Going west out of the Square, you should come to Pikk Street. Continue west until you come to the gate tower once used to keep the local peasants out of Toompea. Go through the gate and climb up along Pikk Jalg Street. At the top you come to Alexander Nevsky Cathedral. Walk round the cathedral to find Toompea Castle. Then walk north along Toom Kooli until you come to Kiriku plats with the Lutheran Cathedral on one side, and the Estonian Art Museum on the other. Take one of the streets on either side of the museum, and you will come to a lookout on the top of the wall that gives a good view of the harbour and the Old Town. Now, retrace your steps to Raekoja plats.

The second trip will take you north. Next to the Town Council Pharmacy is a small alley (Saiakang) which leads to the Church of the Holy Ghost. North-west of the Church is Pikk Street, and here you will find the House of the Great Guild. Continue north-east on Pikk for the House of the Blackheads, St Olaf's Church, the Three Sisters and, finally, the Great Sea Gate and the Maritime Museum.

Start to retrace your steps, but turn right at the Three Sisters (Tolli Street), and then left on Lai Street. Here you will see high-gabled merchants' houses, then turn right on Suur-Kloostri Street to find the Church of the Transfiguration. Turn left on Vaike-Kloostri Street for a good look at the remnants of the city wall, then left on Nunne Street until you come to the gate tower, and then head back to Town Hall Square.

The third trip takes you south from Town Hall Square along Kullaseppa Street to St Nicholas's Church. West of the church is Luhike Street, which heads up to the Adamson-Eric Museum. Come back down and head south and then east on Ruutli Street, and continue east on Muurivahe Street to see Museum of Theatre and Music. Return west to Harju Street. You can now go north on Harju to get back to Town Hall Square, or go south to Vabaduse Valjac.

The fourth trip starts at Vabaduse Valjac, a large open square which is just outside the Old Town Walls. Around the square you will see the Tallinn Art Hall and St John's Church. Go west on Komandandi Street. You will come upon the Virgin Towers, Keik in de Kok, and Lindamagi. Return to the square and walk around the church to Pärnu Street. Going north-east on Pärnu for the Estonian Theatre and Concert Hall. Take a side trip down Osta Street to see the Boy of Bronze. Continue on Pärnu then north on Valli Street to the Viru Gate, then west on Viru Street and back to Town Hall Square.

By now you should be exhausted, so join the locals at one of the cafés in Town Hall Square and have a coffee or beer. Believe it or not, you were never more than 600 m (660 yds) from the Town Hall Square.

1–3 DAYS: SHORT CITY-BREAK

If you have a day or more, and have visited all the Old Town sights, then you can venture into the suburbs of Tallinn. The three trips listed below should each take about half a day.

The top of the list would be Kadriorg Park, which is about 1 km (half a mile) due east of the Old Town. On the way to the park, you can stop at the Anton Hansen Tammsaare Memorial Museum at Koidula 12a. Once you are in the Kadriorg park grounds, see the Eduard Velde Memorial Museum, Kadriorg Palace, Peter the Great's House and the ornamental garden. Just outside the park are the Song Festival Grounds.

A second trip takes you about 2 or 3 km (1.5–2 miles) east of the Old Town and into Pirita. First you will encounter Maarjamae Palace, which now houses part of the Estonian History Museum. In Pirita itself, you will find a huge yachting marina, Pirita Beach and the Botanical Gardens. Be sure to visit the observation platform on the television tower for a great view of Tallinn.

A third trip takes you west to the upmarket suburb of Rocca al Mare, about 6 km (4 miles) west of the Old Town. Here you will find Tallinn Zoo and the Open-air Ethnographic Museum. The area is also home to some of the most expensive real estate in Estonia.

For a full day trip, head to Lahemaa National Park. It is about an hour's drive (70 km/43 miles) east of Tallinn. There is also a regular bus service to the park. The park has a full range of facilities and accommodation. Besides many well-marked hiking and nature trails, there are beach resorts and even a couple of restored palaces.

LONGER: ENJOYING TALLINN TO THE FULL

If you have several days in Tallinn, you may want to take a couple of days to explore the surrounding countryside. The best choice is to go west or south. Although a car is the best way to get around, all places described here have regular bus services from Tallinn.

If you want a few days at a beach resort, then Pärnu, 'Estonia's Summer Capital', is the only place to go (see pages 88–109). The city has a 7 km (4.5 mile) beach, packed with sunbathers in July and August.

For unspoiled landscape you will want to travel to the Estonian Islands in the Baltic, namely Vormsi, Hiiumaa, Saaremaa and Muhu. The islands are sparsely populated, accommodation is minimal, and local public transport is non existent. Plan on taking a car, and, if going in summer, make sure you have reserved accommodation.

For the intellectually minded, a day or two in Tartu (see pages 114–135) is a must. This university town was founded in 1632, and today it is Estonia's main seat of higher learning. The city offers excellent accommodation and facilities.

BEWARE THE STAG WEEKENDERS

With relatively inexpensive flights from London to Tallinn, an increasing number of young British men are flocking to Tallinn for their version of a short city break – weekend stag parties. Tour companies specialising in this type of entertainment lure them with promises of cheap beer and cheap women.

These loud lads show up as groups of drunken louts, staggering from pub to pub, making fools of themselves. Favourite spots of these wandering bands of merrymakers include Molly Malones, Club Havana and McCools. Unless you are planning on joining them, you may want to spend your Friday or Saturday nights in more sophisticated venues.

Something for nothing

Visit the Old Town for the pure joy of immersing yourself for an hour or two wandering the uphill streets of the medieval core of the city. Marvel at the construction of the buildings that has allowed them not only to last the centuries but also to adapt to new uses such as art galleries and cafés.

Tallinn Art Hall and Gallery Some very daring art is to be found inside the very conservative walls of the 1930s building. The smaller exhibit in the Hall is always free, but the main gallery can be seen at no charge on the last day of each temporary exhibit. ❸ Harju 13. ❶ 644 2818. ❷ 12.00–18.00, closed Tues.

City Gallery is known for rapidly changing its exhibits and is noted for its emphasis on contemporary and experimental exhibitions Best of all, it's free. ❸ Harju 13, ❶ 644 28 18. ❷ 12.00–18.00, closed Tuesdays. **Draakoni Gallery** (Dragon's gallery) holds small exhibitions in its beautiful Old Town location (decorated with dragons carved from stone) of local and international artists. ❸ Pikk 18, ❶ 646 41 41. ❷ 10.00–18.00 (closes 17.00 Sat) closed Sun.

National Library of Estonia Yes, you'll find lots and lots of books, newspapers and magazines. This is, after all, a country of rapid readers. However, you'll also find a permanent exhibition of graphic artist Eduard Wilralt's work that is worth seeing. ❸ Tonismagi 2. ❷ 10.00–19.00, closed Sun.

For a free experience you can't beat a fair or a festival. During the summer the streets of Old Town come to life during Old Town Days and the Medieval Market when you'll find locals in period costume.

---

❿ *It costs nothing to browse the Medieval Market, as long as you don't buy…*

When it rains

Become an Estonian and head for a café to drink coffee and discuss how to solve the problems of the world. Then, once you have your caffeine fix you'll have plenty of energy to explore some of the city's museums.

Start with the Tallinn City Museum. Inside a handsomely restored merchant's house you'll find a wonderful collection of the bits and pieces that comprise a history of a city. From medieval costumed figures to posters and photographs, this museum brings the history of Tallinn to life. An added bonus is that much of the exhibit text is in English.

Directly across the street from the City Museum is the Dominican Monastery, once one of the most powerful institutions in Medieval Tallinn. Today it is home to a comprehensive collection of medieval and renaissance stone carvings, including some very intricately carved tombstones.

Still need to burn off some of that caffeine? Head to the Energy Centre (by the harbour ⓐ Pohja pst 29 ⓒ Daily 10.00–17.00) for some hands-on experiences with technology. This museum is filled with some strange looking machinery that may leave you wondering its purpose because not all signs have been translated into English.

If the weather is not only rainy but cold, spend some time in a sauna. Though Estonia's neighbour to the north, Finland, reigns undisputed as the sauna capital of the world, Tallinn does have its fair share of hot spots. There's even a medieval 'Sauna Tower' in Tallinn's Old Town. A lot of hotels and sports clubs in Tallinn have saunas available to rent by the hour. At Kalma, the oldest public bath in Tallinn, a sauna may be taken for between 65-90 krooner, depending on the time of day. If you want a more upmarket sweat try the Meriton Grand Hotel at 800Kr per hour in the evening. Most important, should you drink beer as part of the sauna experience? By all means after you've finished, not before.

Or take yourself off to one of the day spas in Tallinn or nearby Pirita. A spa visit in Estonia can be a bit of pampering, but it's more likely to be a serious adventure in discovering the true state of your health. If you're not keen to discover your current cholesterol level, opt for a soothing massage.

⬤ *There are some hot and steamy venues when it's cold outside*

On arrival

TIME DIFFERENCES

Estonia is 2 hours ahead of Greenwich Mean Time (GMT) and 3 hours ahead during daylight savings.

ARRIVING
By air

With direct flights from 23 cities, Tallinn is easily accessible either by plane or by helicopter. Customs and immigration procedures are usually very quick.

Tallinn's airport is very modern, is user-friendly, is quite small and is not crowded. Car rental companies are on the ground floor, next to the entrance to the car park. It is located just 3 km (2 miles) from the city centre and has excellent facilities, including ATMs, currency exchange, duty-free, restauratnts, tourist information and shops.

From the airport to the city, take bus no. 2, which operates from 07.00–24.00 between the airport, the city centre and the port every 20 mins (every 30 mins Sun), price 15Kr. Tickets can be purchased directly from the bus driver. A taxi from the airport to the city centre should cost about 70Kr.

Tallinn Airport ⓐ Lennujaama tee 2, 11101 Tallinn. ⓣ 605 8888. ⓦ www.tallinn-airport.ee

By rail

There are regular train services from Russia, and from Latvia. Local services run to Tartu and Parnu, but train travel is not a hugely popular form of transport in Estonia.

The rail station is situated near the Old Town and is about 1 km (0.6 miles) from both the city centre and the harbour. There are currency

exchange booths in the train station and ATMs next to the front doors. From the train station to the city centre, take trams 1, 2 or 5, or just walk a couple of hundred metres into the Old Town.
Train Station ⓐ Toompuiestee 37. ① 615 6851. Ⓦ www.evrekspress.ee

By bus

Tallinn is connected by international bus lines to most major cities in Latvia, Lithuania, Russia, Poland and Germany.

The Tallinn Central Bus Terminal is located 1 km (0.6 miles) from the city centre. There is a cash-only currency exchange at the terminal, but its rates are poor. There is an ATM by the main entrance.

Most incoming buses stop at more central locations, such as Viru valjac, before reaching the main terminal. From the bus station to other parts of the city, take trams 2 or 4, or buses 17, 17A or 23. A taxi to the Old Town should cost about 50Kr.
Tallinn Central Bus Terminal ⓐ Lastekodu 46. ① 680 0900.

By car

Tallinn is connected to the rest of Europe by two major highways: Highway 1 (E20) goes east to Russia, and Highway 4 (E67) goes south to Latvia. Entering Estonia from Latvia is quite easy, since both countries are now members of the EU. However, entering from Russia can take a bit of time. In both cases, you will need the car's registration papers and proof of insurance. You can also bring a car in by ferry from Finland or Sweden.

In Estonia, as in the rest of continental Europe, the traffic drives on the right-hand side of the road. Estonian law requires an international driver's licence and a valid insurance policy. During daylight hours, dipped headlights or daytime running lights must be used. After dark, the main headlights must be switched on. The

driver and the passengers must wear seat belts at all times. Petrol stations are easy to find. The largest international chains operating in Estonia are Statoil and Neste.

Both major highways take you right to the centre of town. Traffic is light compared to many cities, so driving into town is easy.

Parking in the city centre and the Old Town area must be paid for. The first 15 minutes of parking are free. A valid parking ticket must be displayed in your windshield from 07.00–19.00 on weekdays and 08.00–15.00 on Saturdays in the city centre. In the Old Town, parking must be paid for 24 hours a day. Tickets are sold by special guards. Guarded and indoor car parks are also available.

By boat

Ferries and catamarans arrive from Finland and Sweden at the Passenger Port, which is less than 1 km (0.6 miles) from the centre of town. The Passenger Port has currency exchange booths and ATMs. A taxi from the port to the centre of town should cost about 40Kr.

Buses 90 and 92 stop here, and can take you into town. Cost is 15Kr. and tickets are available from the driver. A taxi from the port to the centre of town should cost about 40Kr.

FINDING YOUR FEET

The pace of life is generally relaxed in Tallinn. With independence well established, an influx of foreign capital investment, and entry into the EU, the Estonian economy is booming, and Tallinn is the centre of the boom.

Traffic in Tallinn is light compared to other large cities, but the driving tends to be aggressive and definitely not pedestrian friendly. You need to be careful when crossing streets.

Although the overall crime rate is low, petty theft is a problem.

IF YOU GET LOST, TRY ...

Excuse me, do you speak English?
Vabandage, kas te oskate inglise keelt?
Vah-ban-da-ghe, kas teh os-kah-teh ing-li-seh ke-elt?

Excuse me, is this the right way to the old town/the city centre/the tourist office/the station/the bus station?
Kuidas minna raudteejaama/bussijaama/taksopeatusse/kesklinna/(supel)randa?
Kuy-das minnah rowd-te-eh-ya-a-mah/pussy-ya-a-mah/tak-soh-pe-a-tus-seh/kesk-lin-nah/(sup-el-)ran-da?

Can you point to it on my map?
Kas te võite näidata, kus see on kaardi peal?
Kas teh voy-teh nay-da-tah, kus se-e on ka-ar-di pe-al?

I am looking for this address	**I am looking for the . . . hotel**
Ma otsin seda aadressi	Palun, kus on hotell...
Mah ot-sin seh-da a-ad-res-sy	*Pah-loon, kus on hot-tel...*

Stealing from hotel rooms, especially the cheaper ones, is not uncommon. Sneak thieves and pickpockets are also common, especially in areas frequented by tourists. Visitors would be well advised not to carry large sums of cash, and not to flaunt expensive jewellery, cameras or electronic equipment. Such items are better left at home unless really needed.

Theft from cars is common. Tallinn also has its share of muggers,

Rocca
al Mare

Erika

Toostuse

Soo

Niine

Kopli

Sole

Train Station

Pan amae te

Ristiku

OLD TOWN

Toompuieste

Pa^nu Ma

Kaarli Puistee

Estor
Pu

Paldiski Maantee

Tul ka

Luise

Endla

Liivalaia

Mustamae Iee

Endla

Tehnika

Vana-Louna

Veeveri

KRISTINE

B a

Tallinn

Pirita

Song Festival Gardens

ARBOUR

KADRIORG

Joe

Narva Maantee

Gonsiori

Pronksi

Tartu Maantee

Lake Ulemiste

0   500   1000m

so beware of areas that are not well lit, or derelict in appearance, especially at night and near drinking establishments. If possible, do not walk alone.

The exception to normal city life is the Old Town. Here, the narrow winding streets are not conducive to automobiles, and few are present. With most of the Old Town reserved for pedestrians, everything seems to run at a much more leisurely and relaxed pace.

English is quite commonly spoken in Estonia (as in most other European countries), and more Estonians, especially those in international business and those in the tourist industry, are learning to speak it. There is one English-language newspaper in Estonia; the *Baltic Times* is published weekly, and is available at most hotels, some restaurants and many news-stands. Other English-language publications are shipped into Tallinn, and again, are available at most major hotels, and at many news-stands.

ORIENTATION

Tallinn sits on a bay in the Gulf of Finland, about 85 km (52 miles) south of Helsinki. The historic heart of Tallinn, the Old Town is about 1.2 km (1 mile) long by about 1 km (0.6 miles) wide. It sits on a hill overlooking the bay, and for the most part is surrounded by defensive walls built in medieval times.

The skyline of the Old Town is dominated by the spires of several churches and the turrets of Toompea Castle. Reakoja plats (Town Hall Square) is virtually in the geographic centre of the Old Town. The streets of the Old Town radiate outward from Reakoja plats in a rather haphazard fashion.

The main railway station is at the north-west foot of the Old Town, and a short 200 m (660 ft) walk, albeit uphill, puts you inside the Old Town. The main international bus terminal is about 1 km

(0.6 miles) south-east of the Old Town, with regular local bus services directly to the Old Town.

The rest of the 'new' city radiates eastward and westward from the Old Town. A few kilometres east is the suburb of Pirita, while about 6 km (3.5 miles) west is the upmarket suburb of Rocca al Mare, home to the Open-air Ethnographic Museum (see page 94).

GETTING AROUND

Tallinn is a fairly small, compact city, so getting around is quite easy. The centre of town is Viru valjac. It is at the foot of the hill, or dome, upon which Toompea and the Old Town are build, and is also the junction of Highway 1 (Narva Maantee) from the east, and Highway 4 (Pärnu Maantee) from the south.

Toompea, which is built on the top of the hill that dominates Tallinn, is the main city landmark, and easily seen from anywhere in the city. If you get lost, just head for the hill, and in a short time you will be found again.

Many of the points of interest are within one kilometre of Viru valjac, and most are within two kilometres. As the city is pedestrian friendly, walking is the best way to see the city. However, public transport in the form of buses and trams are readily available, at a cost of 15Kr. Note that you can use public transport free a limited number of times if you have a Tallinn Card (see page 6).

Taxis are also available, but be warned that some of them are less than scrupulous. Make sure that the taxi has a visible meter, that it works, and that the driver starts it. The driver should also have his registration, complete with photograph and stamps, prominently displayed. The cost of a taxi from one point to another within the city centre should cost no more than 70Kr.

Rental cars are available, but are not recommended unless one is

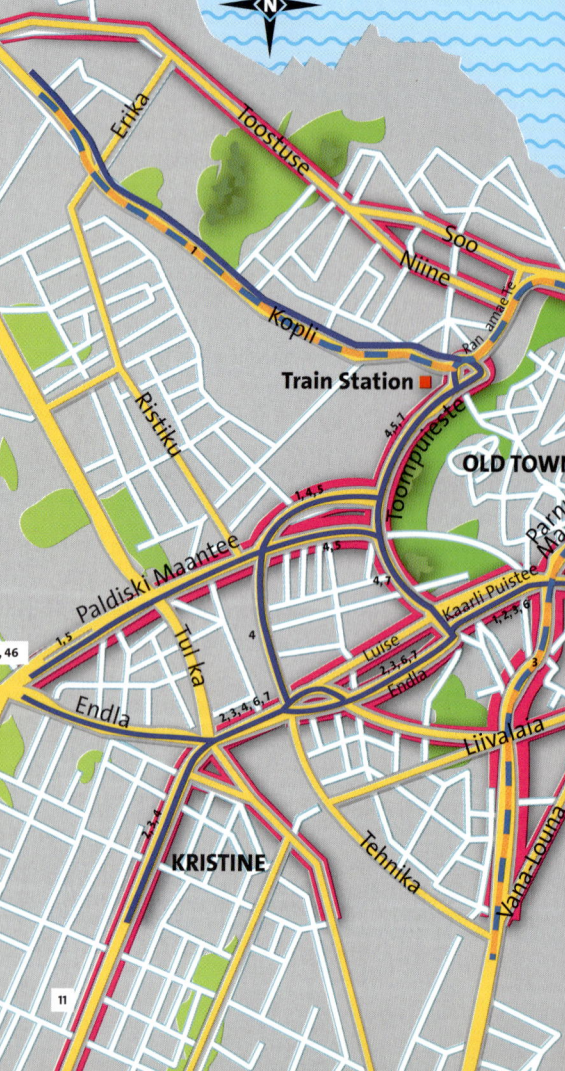

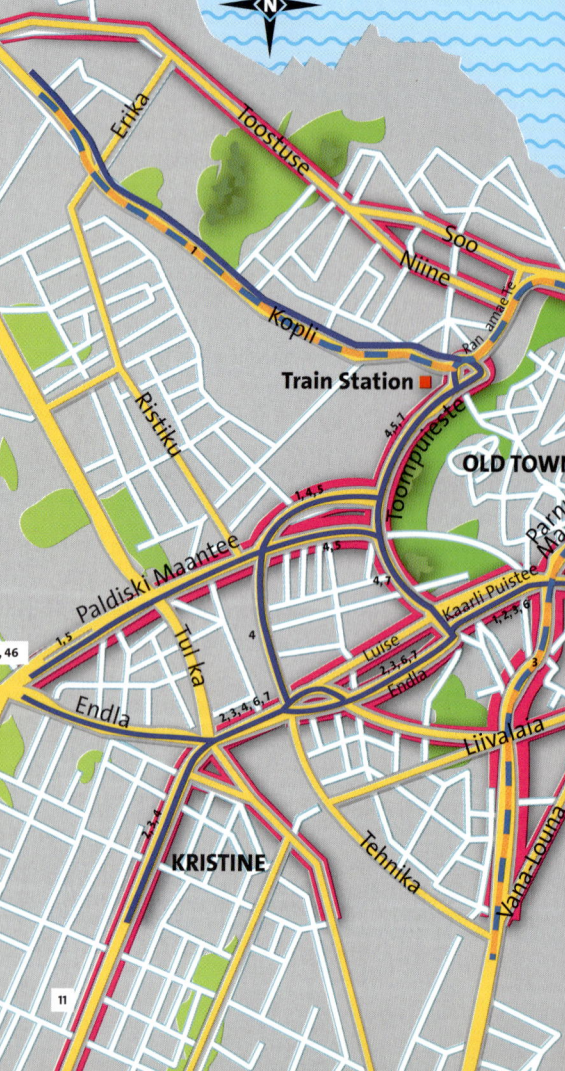

Legend

- Tramway
- Trolley bus
- Bus route
- Bus terminus

The nearest bus terminus to the Old Town is Viru Keskus. Only bus services to and from Viru Keskus are shown on this map; numbers shown in boxes.

1, 8, 34A, 38

19, 29, 33, 44, 51, 53, 56, 60, 63, 68

31, 67

14, 18, 36

Bay of Tallinn

HARBOUR

Ahtri

Joe

u Keskus

Narva Maantee

KADRIORG

Gonsiori

Pronksi

Tartu Maantee

0   500   1000m

planning to travel outside the city. Getting around on foot, by public transport, or even by taxi, is easier and less costly.

CAR HIRE

Unless you are planning on visiting locations outside of Tallinn, renting a car is not recommended. The city is compact enough, with most of the attractions close enough in, that walking, using the public transport, or even hiring taxis, is much more economical and practical. Also, parking is hard to find, and expensive. Most of the major car rental agencies are represented in Tallinn, both at the airport, and in the city centre. You can expect to pay the same prices as in Western Europe. There are some local car rental companies that can be cheaper than the major renters, but the mechanical condition of the car may be questionable.

Some major car rental agencies are:
Avis ⓐ Liivalaia 13/15. ❶ 667 1515. ❶ 08.00–17.00 Mon–Fri.
ⓦ www.avis.ee
Budget ⓐ Tallinn airport. ❶ 605 8600. ⓔ airport@budget.ee.
❶ Daily 09.00–18.00 ⓦ www.budget.ee
Europcar ❶ At the airport, ❶ 605 8031, ⓔ europcar@europcar.ee.
ⓦ www.europcar.ee
Hertz ⓐ Tallinn airport. ❶ 605 8923 ⓔ airport@hertz.ee ❶ Daily
09.00–18.00. ⓦ www.hertz.ee
National ❶ Tallinn Airport. ❶ 605 8071 ⓔ carental@online.ee.
❶ Daily 09.00–18.00. ⓦ www.nationalcar.ee

⏵ *Town hall square – Raekoja plats – is at the heart of the city*

The Old Town

The city of Tallinn has had a turbulent past. Much of the time the city has either been under siege or lived with the threat of invasion. To cope, the residents built massive walls to surround the town. With some 46 towers, medieval Tallinn was possibly the most fortified town in all of Northern Europe. Today only 20 towers and not quite 2 km (1.5 miles) of the walls remain. A few of the towers, such as Fat Margaret and Kiek in de Kok, serve as museums. But a great many have been transformed into restaurants, hotels, homes and offices. The oldest of the towers, Nunne, Sauna and Kuldjala, remain open to the public.

The Old Town may appear compact on the map, but you can spend hours, if not days, exploring its intriguing nooks and crannies. Your adventure afoot will give you a glimpse of life in Tallinn. From up-and-coming entrepreneurs who can afford to renovate ancient buildings, to the ageing ladies who come to beg outside the Lutheran cathedral, the Old Town is Tallinn of yesterday and today.

The joy of sightseeing in the Old Town area of Tallinn is that it is comfortably walkable. The narrow, twisted, and sometimes quite vertically inclined streets allow for minimal automobile traffic, and no public transport.

SIGHTS & ATTRACTIONS

Town Hall and Town Hall Square

Raekoja plats (Town Hall Square) is as old as Tallinn itself. Surrounded by medieval buildings painted in pastel colours, the square is a landmark of the country, and a popular rallying point for Estonian patriotism. On the south side stands the Town Hall, built in the 15th century. Look up to see the Gothic arches, steeple and

OLD TOWN

- Great Sea Gate
- Maritime Museum
- St Olaf's Church
- Toll
- The Three Sisters
- Linomuseum
- Dominican Monasteries
- House of the Blackheads
- Estonia History Museum
- St Nicholas's Church
- Toompark
- Church of the Holy Ghost
- Kirilai Plots
- Raekoja Plats
- Town Hall
- Toompea
- Museum of Photography
- Niguliste
- Lossi Platz
- Toompea Hill
- Cathedral
- Toompea Castle
- Kiek in de Kok
- Muurivahe
- Falgi tee
- Komandandi
- Tallin Art Hall
- Train Station

Streets: Soo, Niine, Rannamae Te, Suurtuki, Lai, Pikk, Ahtri, Nunne, Suur-Kloostri, Rataskaevu, Pikk Jalg, Lunik, Dunkri, Vene, Viru, Kuni, Suur-Karja, Vaike-Karja, Parnu Maatee, Estonia Puiestee, Falgi tee, Kaarli Puestee, Luise, Endla, Liivalaia, To mpuieste

Scale: 0 — 250 — 500m

A SPOT OF BOTHER

Look for two long cobblestones that form the letter 'L' in a corner of the Town Hall Square near the Raeapteek. This marks the location where a priest was beheaded, on the spot, for having killed a waitress who brought food not to his liking. You may not want to tip your waitress but be careful not to cause her any harm.

weather vane. Note the green painted dragons just below the roof line; they spout water rather than breathe fire.

🅐 Raekoja plats 1. 🕿 645 7900. 🆆 www.tallinn.ee/raekoda

Town Hall Pharmacy (Raeapteek)

One of the oldest continuously running pharmacies in Europe is on Town Hall Square. Records exist showing it dates back to at least 1422, but it could have opened even earlier than that. In medieval times the ailing could buy burnt bees and bat powder for treatments, and if you didn't have a specific ailment you could buy a glass of spiced claret. The pharmacy offers modern medications these days, but a part of the store is a museum.

🅐 Raekoja plats 11. 🕿 631 4860. 🕑 09.00–19.00 Mon–Fri; 09.00–17.00 Sat; 09.00–16.00 Sun.

Alexander Nevsky Cathedral

Built in 1900, this relative newcomer does not quite fit architecturally into the rest of the medieval Old Town. A typical

⏵ *The cathedral is a reminder of the Russian influence on the country*

onion-domed Russian Orthodox Church, it sits next to the Toompea Castle and can be seen from most parts of the city. Inside is an impressive display of religious icons.

ⓐ Lossi plats 10. ☎ 644 3484. ⏱ Daily 08.00–19.00.
ⓦ www.hot.ee/nsobor.

Toompea Castle

Sitting at the very top of Toompea, the hill that overlooks the city, Toompea Castle stands as a sentry that for most of Tallinn's history has guarded the city. It was an Estonian stockade until captured by the Danes in 1219. The Danes built the first stone castle, and the castle has been rebuilt and renovated many times since, the latest by Russia's Catherine the Great, who gave it the current pink baroque facade. It is dominated by three defensive towers, the tallest of which, 'Tall Herman', dates from 1371, and proudly flies the Estonian flag. Admission only with guided tour.

ⓐ On Toompea Hill. Admission only with guided tour.

Church of the Holy Ghost

Built in the 1360s, this is the only church in Tallinn whose exterior remains in its original form. Many historic events happened here. The clock was set into the wall in 1680, and is the oldest timepiece in Estonia. Although simple and humble on the outside, the interior is richly decorated and contains precious works of medieval art.

ⓐ Pühavaimu 2 ⏱ Mon–Fri 10.00–15.00 (and Sat in summer).

Estonian History Museum

Housed in the Great Guild Hall, the museum's exhibitions cover

---

⬤ *House of the Blackheads – even if you don't go inside, the exterior will impress*

Estonia's earliest history up to the 18th century, with explanations translated into English. The building itself (built 1407–1410) was a gathering place for Tallinn's wealthy merchants.

📍 Pikk 17. ☎ 641 1630. 🌐 www.eam.ee 🕐 Daily 11.00–18.00; closed Wed. Admission charge.

House of the Blackheads

The Brotherhood of the Blackheads was a merchants' guild founded in 1343, and the house was built as lodgings for visiting merchants. Although initially run with the best of intentions, over the centuries it degenerated into a social drinking club, finally dissolving in 1940 when the Russians moved in. The house is elaborately decorated in Renaissance style, both inside and out. Not normally open to the public, you can see the interior if you attend one of the regularly scheduled chamber concerts.

📍 Pikk 26. ☎ 631 3199. 🌐 www.mustpeademaja.ee

St Olaf's Church (Oleviste Kirik)

The spire of this church is Tallinn's landmark. At one time it may have been the tallest spire in all of Europe, some say. Although the church dates from 1267, the interior is from the 1840s and reflects the style of that day.

📍 Pikk 48. ☎ 641 2241. 🌐 www.oleviste.ee 🕐 Daily 10.00–14.00.

The Three Sisters

This luxury hotel, built into three famous medieval houses on the end of Pikk tänav, provides the quintessential Tallinn experience. The top-notch establishment offers large rooms decorated in a striking blend of modern and antique styles. Flatscreen TVs can be found alongside old-fashioned bathtubs, and hidden staircases and walkways link the three buildings. The library with fireplace and cosy wine cellar are nice extras. ⓐ Pikk 71/Tolli 2. ⓣ 630 6300. ⓦ www.threesistershotel.com

Great Sea Gate

At the very northern end of the Old Town, the Great Sea Gate is a 16th-century arch flanked by two towers. The larger of the two towers is 'Fat Margaret'. This barrel-shaped tower has walls 4 m (13 ft) thick, and, when no longer needed for defensive purposes, became the city's jail. Fat Margaret now houses the Estonian Maritime Museum.

ⓐ Pikk 70. ⓣ 641 1408. ⓛ 10.00–18.00 Wed–Sun; closed public holidays.

Maritime Museum

Tallinn's significant seafaring history is put on display in this museum housed over four floors of the 16th-century Fat Margaret cannon tower. Don't miss the antique diving equipment or the spectacular views from the roof.

ⓐ Fat Margaret Tower, Pikk 70. ⓣ 641 1408. ⓛ Daily 10.00–18.00; closed Mon–Tues. Admission charge, ⓦ www.meremuuseum.ee

Church of the Transfiguration

Originally belonging to St Michael's Convent of the Cistercian Order (located next door and now housing the Gustavus Adolphus School), the church was given to an Orthodox congregation in 1716. The church has retained its original form, save the addition of a baroque spire in 1776 and exterior renovations in the early 1800s. The carved-wood iconostasis is one of the most impressive of its kind. ⓐ Suur-Kloostri 14-1. ⓣ 646 4003.

St Nicholas's Church

Started in the 13th century and rebuilt in the 15th century, this imposing church is now a museum which holds Tallinn's collection of medieval art. There are several carved and painted altars, friezes, tomb-top effigies, and other interesting works. The church's pipe organ pumps out music on Saturdays and Sundays, late in the afternoon.

The present classical building dates from the 1820s, but a Russian Orthodox church stood here in the early 1400s. The young church houses many objects of artistic value predating it, including 16th-century icons.

ⓐ Vene 24. ☎ 644 1945. 🕐 Mon–Sun 09.30–17.00. Services Sat 09.30 and 18.00, Sun 10.00.

St John's Church

A pseudo-Gothic church built for a local Lutheran congregation, St John's boasts the first bell (dating from 1872) inscribed in Estonian.
ⓐ Vabaduse väljak 1. ☎ 644 6206. 🕐 Daily 10.00–17.00, closed Mon. Services Sun at 10.00

Kiek in de Kok (Peep into the Kitchen)

This combination tower and museum provides an excellent introduction to the history of Tallinn's elaborate defence system of walls and towers. Built between 1475–1481, the 38m (120ft) six-storey cannon tower was partly destroyed in the Livonian War of 1558–1583. Ivan IV's army left nine cannonballs embedded in the tower's walls. Three floors of the tower, restored to its 17th-century appearance, are galleries showing of contemporary art. The tower's

---

▶ *It is easy to spot which of the towers is 'Fat Margaret'*

unusual name comes from the vantage point it offers if you climb to the top of its stairs.

ⓐ Komandandi 2. ☎ 644 6686. ⓦ www.linnamuuseum.ee/ kiekindekok. ⏰ Daily 10.30–18.00; closed Mon.

Boy of Bronze

Originally erected in 1947, this controversial monument in front of the National Library commemorated Soviet soldiers who died fighting in World War II, and, from the point of view of locals, occupying Estonia. It served as a kind of 'tomb of the unknown soldier', at one point having an 'eternal flame' burning in front. After the Soviet Union fell, the monument was one of the few of its kind to survive, mainly due to efforts by the local Russian-speaking population.

The plaques that now flank the soldier simply read 'For those fallen in World War II' with no reference to nationality.

ⓐ Tõnismägi 2

Tallinn City Museum (Linnamuuseum)

Built into a 14th-century merchant house, this museum manages to compact centuries of the city's history into a complete and lively array of exhibits. Most of the exhibits have English captions.

ⓐ Vene 17. ☎ 644 6553. ⓦ www.linnamuuseum.ee
⏰ Daily 10.30–18.00; closed Tues.

Dominican Monastery

One of Tallinn's oldest existing buildings, this monastery was founded 1246. The part of the monastery administered by the museum includes the courtyard and surrounding passageways, where fascinating 15th- and 16th-century stone carvings are on

display. To see the inner rooms, visit the Claustrum, listed below.
🅰 Vene 16. ❶ 644 4606. Ⓦ www.kloostri.ee
🕒 Daily 09.30–18.00. Admission charge.

Dominican Monastery Claustrum

The monastery's inner chambers, such as the monk's dormitory,
priory, library, etc., can only be visited as part of an organised tour.
One of the most interesting spots may be the downstairs room that
houses the 'energy pillar' purportedly the source of a mysterious
power. 🅰 Muurivahe 33. ❶ 644 6530.
Ⓦ www.mauritanum.edu.ee
🕒 Daily 10.00–17.00. Admission charge.

CULTURE

To find out what will be on to book tickets for concerts in the city
see Ⓦ www.concert.ee/english/tallinn/concerts/

Estonia Concert Hall

The number-one place to hear classical music and operatic
performances. 🅰 Estonia pst 4. ❶ 614 7760.

Estonian National Opera

This company has its home at the Estonia Concert Hall.
🅰 Estonia pst. 4. ❶ 683 1201.

Niguliste Museum and Concert Hall

This 13th-century Gothic church holds regular organ concerts. While
there, you can also see a fascinating collection of medieval art.
🅰 Niguliste 3. ❶ 631 4340.

House of the Brotherhood of the Blackheads

This gloriously ornate guildhall (see page 70) plays hosts to classical music concerts nearly every night. It also hosts monthly social dance soirees, so be sure to get a copy of the events calendar. ❸ Pikk 26. ❶ 631 3199.

Knighthood House

This grand building perched on Toompea hill serves as the main branch of the Art Museum of Estonia. The collection provides an excellent overview of Estonian art. ❸ Kiriku plats 1. ❶ 644 9340. ❸ 11.00–18.00; closed Mon and Tues. Admission charge.

Adamson-Eric Museum

The permanent collection of works by world-famous artist Adamson-Eric is housed in a 16th-century building within the Old Town. ❸ Luhikejaig 3. ❶ 644 5838. ❸ 11.00–18.00; closed Mon and Tues. Admission charge (free with Tallinn Card).

Museum of Photography

Today this former city prison (14th century) houses a compact exhibition on Estonian photography. The first camera arrived in Tallinn just one year after debuting in France and the art developed quickly. Don't miss the contemporary exhibitions and shop. ❸ City Prison, Raekoja tänav 4/6. ❶ 644 6553. ❿ www.linnamuuseum.ee ❸ Daily 10.30–18.00; closed Tues. Admission charge (free with Tallinn card).

---

❶ *Flowers aren't just saved for special occasions in Tallinn*

RETAIL THERAPY

Tallinn is not a destination for the avid shopper. However, if you are looking for a special souvenir, the streets of the Old Town are the place to shop. Linen, wool clothing and amber jewellery are local specialities, and you will find these at many shops, especially along Pikk and Dunkri. The best place for woollens is the open-air woollen market on Muurivahe just north of Viru Gate.

Most stores are open Mon–Fri from 10.00–17.00. Shops close early on Sat and may not be open at all on Sun. However, since this is a prime area for tourists you're likely to find a good selection of shops that can't resist catering to visitors.

Speciality and souvenir shops
Galerli Prints, greetings cards and paintings by local artists. ⓐ Vanaturu kael 3.

Jardin Souvenirs, woollens, linen and wooden utensils. ⓐ Apteegi 3.

Katerlina Guild Several craft workshops along Catherine's passage. Ceramics, leatherwork, stained glass and jewellery. ⓐ Vene 12.

Keraamika Atelje Rather artsy ceramic creations. Wonderful, but strange. ⓐ Pikk 33.

Kodukasitoo National costumes, linen and handicrafts. ⓐ Muurivahe 17.

Kuld ja Hobeehted Tea sets designed by Adamson-Eric. Also ceramics, jewellery and glassware. ⓐ Pikk 27.

Puupood Everything here is made of wood. ❸ Lai 5.

Veta Probably the best linens in town. Tablecloths and clothes are best. ❸ Pikk 4.

Zizi Ethnographic textiles for the home. ❸ Vene 12.

Meloodia Specialising in local contemporary classical composers. ❸ Kuninga 4.

Apollo Bookstore Lots of novels and guidebooks in English. Upstairs the café has cushy sofas to plonk into to peruse your new purchase while sipping a gourmet coffee. ❸ Viru 23. ❶ Mon–Fri 10.00–20.00; Sat 10.00–18.00 ; Sun 11.00–16.00.

Draakoni Gallery This quaint gallery (see page 48) also houses a shop where you can buy works of art. ❸ Pikk 18. ❶ 646 4110. ❶ Daily 10.00–17.00; closed Sun.

TAKING A BREAK

Pitstop It's got almost everything a tourist's heart could desire – internet, billiards, karaoke, singing proprietor and clean washrooms. ❸ Viru 11. ❶ 669 1510. ❶ 669 1513. ❶ www.vanawiru.ee ❶ Daily 08.00–02.00.

Hesburger An outpost of the Finnish hamburger chain. ❸ Viru 27. ❶ 627 2516. ❶ Daily 09.00–23.00; 09.00–23.00 Fri; 09.00–01.00 Sat.

Bogapott Hidden away in a part of the medieval town wall on

Toompea, here you'll find pastries, sandwiches and an art shop with a ceramics studio. ❷ Pikk jalg 9. ❶ 631 3181. Ⓦ www.bogapott.ee
🕒 Daily 10.00–18.00.

Café Anglais A favourite of Tallinn's foreign community. Could it be the friendly atmosphere? The fresh salads? Or possibly the best cup of coffee in the city? ❷ Raekoja plats 14. ❶ 644 2160. 🕒 Daily 11.00–23.00.

Chocolaterie Café Quaint, pretty and in need of a lot more chairs. A master chocolatier makes truffles from scratch. Just the sugar hit you'll need to carry on sightseeing. ❷ Vene 6 (in the courtyard). ❶ 641 8061. 🕒 Daily 10.00–23.00.

Elsebet Eat in, or take back to your hotel some of the best pastries in Tallinn. Since your bag of goodies probably won't make it back to the hotel, take a seat at one of the restaurant's candle-lit wooden tables. ❷ Viru 2. ❶ 646 6800. Ⓦ www.peppersack.ee 🕒 Daily 08.00–24.00.

Kibuvits Good spot to have lunch or just kick back and read a newspaper while you have a nosh and listen to the jazz from the stereo. ❷ Uus 19. ❶ 641 2096. ❻ 641 2033. 🕒 Daily 10.00–21.00.

AFTER DARK

Kompressor Students love the simple decor, oversized tables and cheap drinks. Add to that the good and incredibly cheap pancakes, and you've got the makings of a budget night out. ❷ Rataskaevu 3. ❶ 646 4210. 🕒 Daily 11.00–23.00; 11.00–02.00 Fri–Sun.

Kolumbus Krisostomus It can be filled with tourists doing karaoke, but this beer hall type pub does host some of the more interesting local bands. ⓐ Viru 24, 2nd floor. ⓣ 5615 6924 . ⓦ www.kolumbus.ee ⓛ Mon–Thur 11.00–24.00, Fri–Sat 12.00–01.00.

Scotland Yard For decor, we've got an old English sitting room, that's been enlarged about 20 times, with a police theme. For all its pastiche it still attracts some of the largest weekend crowds. ⓐ Mere pst. 6e. ⓣ 653 51 90. ⓦ www.scotlandyard.ee ⓛ Mon–Wed 12.00–24.00, Thur–Sat 12.00–03.00.

Von Krahli Baar The local students call it call it 'the Krahl.' If you don't favour the sounds of alternative bands come by for the cheap, good food during the day. ⓐ Rataskaevu 10/12. ⓣ 626 9096. ⓦ www.vonkrahl.ee ⓛ Mon–Thur 12.00–01.00; Fri–Sat 12.00–03.00.

Valli Baar At first glance this Old Town pub doesn't look worthy of a second glance. But at night, when students drop in for cheap drinks and irregular elderly regulars start to swing to the live accordion music, the atmosphere moves into the realm of the surreal. ⓐ Muurivahe 14. ⓣ 641 8379. ⓛ Daily 11.00–23.00.

Karoliina Shaped like a tunnel and dug into a hillside of the Old Town this is a great location for a quiet tete-a-tete, or quiet catch up with some friends. ⓐ Harju 6. ⓛ Daily 11.00–22.00.

St Patrick's Part of a small chain, it may look and sound Irish but the clientele is Estonian. The food is good and every fourth Saku Originaal is free. ⓐ Suur-Karja 8. ⓣ 641 8173. ⓦ www.patricks.ee ⓛ Sun–Thur 11.00–02.00, Sat 11.00–04.00.

City Centre

Truly, there is more to Tallinn than just the Old Town. Once outside of that compact area you'll discover a modern city humming with activity and populated with familiar global signage from Radisson to 7–11. As with all contemporary cities you'll find the focus to be more on business rather than sightseeing. But there are just enough galleries and museums to keep your interest level high.

SIGHTS & ATTRACTIONS

Rotermann Salt Storage
Once used to store salt, this faithfully restored limestone warehouse is now home to the Estonian Museum of Architecture, and provides exhibition space for the Museum of Art. A few mins' walk from the Old Town.
ⓐ Ahtri 2. ⓣ 625 7000. ⓛ 11.00–18.00; closed Mon and Tues. Admission charge.

A. H. Tammsaare Museum
Anton Hansen Tammsaare (1878–1940) is generally considered to be the greatest Estonian writer of the 20th century. His most famous work is the five-part epic, *Truth and Justice*, which covers all strata of Estonian society. The museum chronicles his life and work, but just as interesting is the apartment, painstakingly restored to its 1930s original, where the writer lived his last eight years.
ⓐ L. Koidula 12A. ⓣ 601 3232. ⓦ www.vilde.tammsaare.ee/ tammsaare.php. ⓛ Wed–Sun 11.00–17.00. Admission charged (but free with Tallinn card). ⓝ It is easily accessible by trams nos. 1 and 3 from the central part of Tallinn

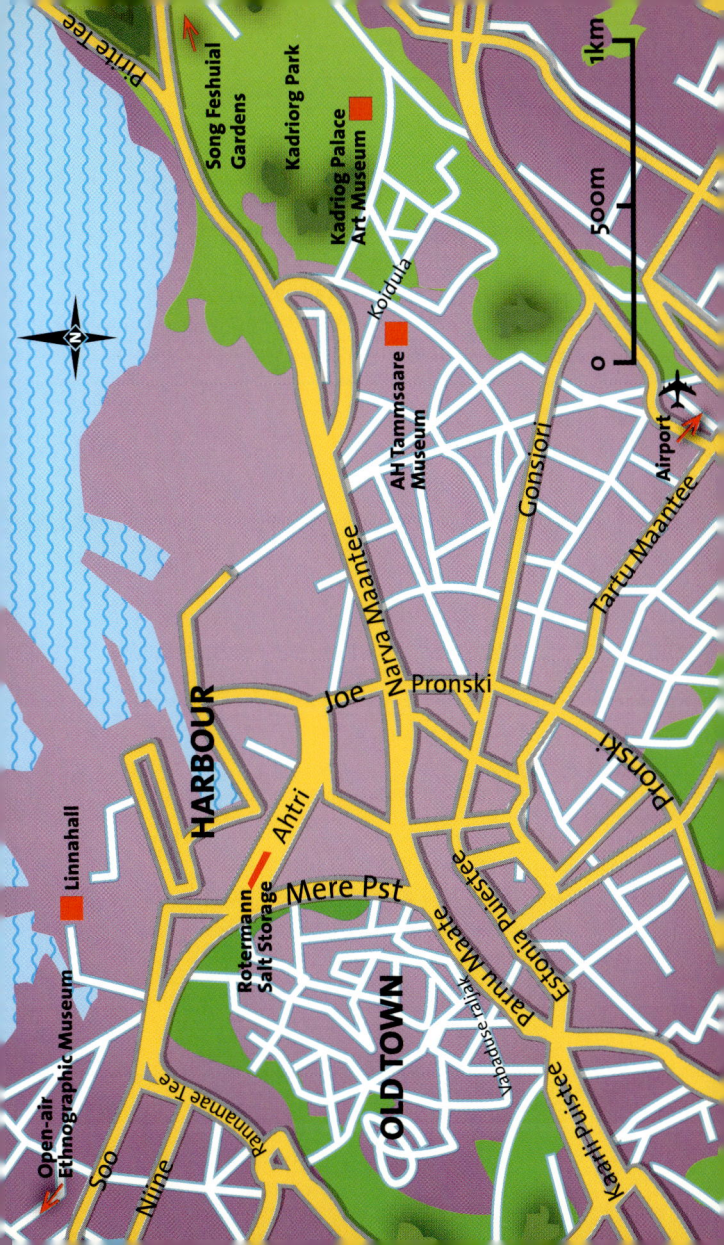

Pirite Tee

Song Feshuial Gardens

Kadriorg Park

Kadriog Palace Art Museum

Koidula

AH Tammsaare Museum

Gonsiori

Airport

Tartu Maantee

Pronski

Narva Maantee

Joe

Pronski

HARBOUR

Ahtri

Linnahall

Rotermann Salt Storage

Mere Pst

Estonia Puiestee

Parnu Maarte

Vabaduse Valjak

Kaarli Puistee

OLD TOWN

Open-air Ethnographic Museum

Soo

Niine

Pannamae Tee

N

1km

500m

0

CULTURE

Tallinn Art Hall and Gallery (Tallinna Kunstihoone)

Inside this imposing 1930s building you'll discover avant-garde and daring exhibitions from Estonia and abroad. ⓐ Vabaduse valjak 8. ⓣ 644 2818. ⓛ 12.00–18.00; closed Tues. Admission charge, except for the last day of exhibitions (see page 48). ⓝ Trolley 1, 2, 3, 6.

Linnahall

This great grey monolith at the edge of the harbour plays host to pop concerts and big-name artists. ⓐ Mere pst. 20. ⓣ 641 1500. ⓝ Tram 1, 2; bus no. 3.

Saku Suurhall

This concert and sports arena is best known for hosting the Eurovision Song Contest in 2002. The venue holds a range of events and has its own sports bar and restaurant. ⓐ Paldiski mnt. 104. ⓣ 660 0200. ⓝ Trolley (nos 6, 7); buses (nos 21, 22).

RETAIL THERAPY

Tallinn is served by two large department stores: **Stockmann**, ⓐ Liivalaia 53, and **Tallinna Kaubamaja**, ⓐ Gonsiori 2.
Rahva Raamat Maps, some English-language novels. ⓐ Pärnu mnt. 38.

Lasering Estonian and international rock and pop CDs and DVDs – everything from indie to film soundtracks. ⓐ Pärnu mnt. 38.

ⓞ *Contrasting old and new building styles in the city centre*

AFTER DARK

Vana Villemi Pubi Typical Estonian pub decor with lots of wood, and it has leather sofas to sink into. Old Villem is slightly off the beaten track so doesn't draw large numbers of tourists. Soak up the country-style ambience or just soak up some beer and get raucous with everyone else. ⓐ Tartu mnt. 52. ⓣ 637 6178. ⓦ www.vanavillem.ee ⓛ Daily 11.00–24.00.

Café Peterson This warm, stylish little café has a definite air of culture. Not only is it attached to an art gallery, it's also frequented by students from the neighbouring Tallinn Pedagogical University. Stop in for quiche, or for the live piano music on Friday nights. ⓐ Narva mnt. 15. ⓣ 662 2195. ⓦ www.cafepeterson.ee ⓛ Mon–Sat 09.00–23.00; Sun 10.00–22.00.

Café Carlos This bright café serves everything from patisserie and bacon-and-egg type combinations to tapas and enchiladas. ⓐ Pronksi 3. ⓣ 640 3944; ⓦ cafe.carlos.ee ⓛ Mon–Fri 08.00–21.00; Sat–Sun 11.00–21.00.

The Englishman Pub Serving English beer and playing English music, this is not bad at all for a hotel pub. The decor is a cross between a cricket museum and a gentlemen's club, with English newspapers and magazines available, but that doesn't prevent the nightlife from becoming downright raucous. ⓐ Reval Hotel Olümpia, Liivalaia 33. ⓣ 631 5831. ⓦ www.revalhotels.com ⓛ Sun–Thur 16.00–01.00; Fri–Sat 16.00–03.00.

ⓞ *Even Saku Suurhall has its own sports bar*

Bar Bogart Dedicated to the memory of Bogey, which is quite surprising for a bar that now puts the emphasis on dancing, though it used to be known more as a whisky bar with occasional showings of *Casablanca*. Plays mainly dance music to fill the dancefloor and, if you must have it, karaoke. ⓐ Sokos Hotel Viru, Viru väljak 4. ⓣ 680 9380. ⓕ 680 9236. ⓦ www.viru.ee ⓛ Tues–Sat 11.00–03.00; Sun–Mon 11.00–23.00 .

Suburbs East & West

KADRIORG & PIRITA

KADRIORG

Kadriorg is a large public park about 1 km (0.6 mile) east of the Old Town. Created by Tsar Peter the Great in the early 18th century, the heavily forested park is criss-crossed with paths, and dotted with statues, ponds and fountains. In the centre is the magnificent Kadriorg Palace. The park contains other historic and important buildings, such as Peter the Great's House, the Estonian Presidential Palace, and several other museums.

Kadriorg Palace Art Museum

Once a palace belonging to Peter the Great, the outside of this building is a work of art in itself. The Palace plays host to Estonia's museum of foreign art, with works by German, Italian and Dutch masters. Most of the collection, however, is devoted to 18th- and 19th-century Russian painters. There are also collections of porcelain, sculpture and glassworks. ❸ Weizenbergi 37. ❶ 606 6400. ❺ 10.00–17.00; closed Mon and Tues, public holidays. Admission charge.

Kadriorg Art Museum

Peter I began building the palace in 1718, named Ekaterinenthal, or Catherinenthal, in honour of Catherine I. Currently, the baroque Kadriorg Palace houses the foreign art collection of the Estonian Art Museum. The collection contains more than 900 Western European and Russian paintings from the 16th to the 20th centuries, about 3500 prints, over 3000 sculptures and gems, and about 1600

TV Tower & Botanical Gardens

St Bridget's Convert

PIRITA

Pirita Tee

Song Festival Grounds

Narva Mnt

Narva Mnt

Kadriorg Park

A. Weizenbergi

Kodriorg Palace/ Art Museum

Mikkel Museum

Gonsiori

Laagna Tee

Peterburi Tee

0   500m   1km

N

decorative arts objects (historical furniture, porcelain, glass, etc.). The upper flower garden, behind the palace, has been reconstructed in 18th-century style, and is open to visitors in the summer. The café and museum shop are open during museum opening hours.

ⓐ A. Weizenbergi 37. ❶ 606 6400. Admission charge (but free with Tallinn card). Ⓝ From the city centre it is the best to take tram 1 or 3 to the final stop where it is a few minutes' walk to the palace.

Kadriorg Park

One of the most popular places in the park is the symmetrical Swan Lake and its surroundings. Only a small part of the large park was designed as a formal park in its time – most of it was intended to preserve the look of the natural landscape. Lining the promenade leading from Swan Lake to the palace (Weizenbergi Street) are many of the palace's auxiliary buildings. The restoration workshop of the Estonian Art Museum is located in the palace's guest house and the park pavilion next door. Opposite the palace gates is a small guard house, the palace's kitchen building and ice cellar.

Mikkel Museum

Johannes Mikkel donated his substantial collection of Chinese, Russian and European paintings, prints, icons and porcelain to the Estonian Art Museum in 1994. The collection is now housed in the renovated kitchen building in the grounds of the Kadriorg Palace. ⓐ Weizenbergi 28. ❶ 644 6873. 🕐 11.00–18.00; closed Mon and Tues. Ⓝ From the city center it is the best to take tram 1 or 3 to the final stop where it is a few minutes' walk to the museum.

▶ *The home of Peter the Great now houses an art museum*

PIRITA

This seaside suburb is located 6 km (3.5 miles) from Tallinn's city
centre. In the early 20th century, the town of Pirita began to develop
into a destination for Sunday rides and swimming. Today Pirita is
one of the favourite places in Tallinn for spending free time, with its
bathing beaches, coastline, pine-forested parks and picturesque
Pirita River valley. Tallinn's Botanical Gardens has lands on either side
of the Pirita River, near the TV Tower. To get to Pirita, take bus no. 34
or 38 from the main post office.

Tallinn TV Tower

The 314 m (343 yd) TV Tower was built for the 1980 Olympic Games.
From 170 m (560 ft) you can get a gorgeous view of Tallinn. There's a
restaurant on the same floor as the observation tower for longer
gazing. ⓐ Kloostrimetsa tee 58A. ① 600 5511. ⓦ www.teletorn.ee.
🕐 Daily 10.00–22.00. Ⓝ Bus 34a, 38.

Botanical Gardens

Located in Pirita, near the TV Tower, the gardens feature virtually
every type of tree and plant found in Estonia. The grounds are
immaculately kept, and in the centre is a Palm House (where they
hold changing exhibitions), a rose garden and an alpine garden.
ⓐ Kloostrimetsa tee 52. ① 602 2666. Ⓝ Take bus no. 34A or 38 from
Viru keskus to Kloostrimetsa stop. 🕐 Daily 11.00–16.00 (glasshouses);
gardens open till 19.00 in summer.

St Bridget's Convent

Established by Tallinn's wealthy merchants in 1407, the church was

▶ *St Bridget's Convent is possibly linked to Tallinn by secret passages*

destroyed in the second half of the 16th century, and only the western limestone gable, 35 m (115 ft) high, and side walls remain. In the 17th century, a farmers' cemetery developed in front of the ruins. There are tales of secret underground passageways between the convent and the city. ⓐ Kloostri tee 9. ⓣ 605 5044. ⓛ Mon and Sun 10.00–16.00. Admission charge, free with Tallinn card. ⓝ Take bus no. 1, 8, 34, 38 or 99 from Viru väljak to Pirita stop.

Song Festival Grounds
This is where the 'Singing Revolution' (see page 22) began in 1988. The Lauluvaijak is comprised of both a huge outdoor arena and a modern indoor concert hall. ⓐ Narva mnt. 95. ⓣ 611 2100.

AFTER DARK

Buldogi's Pub Pub, serving food, that has live music events and shows European football matches ⓐ Jaama 2 Nõmme. ❶ 650 4123. ⓦ www.buldogipub.ee ⓛ Daily 10.00–24.00; Thur–Sat 10.00–01.00.

Kamikaze Serves typical pub food. ⓐ Sõstra 2. ❶ 656 7878. ⓦ www.kamikaze.ee ⓛ Daily 11.00–24.00; Fri–Sat 11.00–02.00.

Lydia €€€ Next to Kadriorg Park, this restaurant has live music Thurs–Sat evenings to accompany the fine dining it offers. Serves Estonian specialities for lunch and dinner. ⓐ Koidulatn 13a ❶ 626 8990. ⓦ www.lydia.ee ⓛ Daily 12.00–23.00 (closes at 19.00 on Sun).

OPEN-AIR ETHNOGRAPHIC MUSEUM

Located on the western outskirts of Tallinn, this museum brings together over 100 village buildings of the 18th and 19th centuries from around Estonia. Exhibits illustrate how the villagers lived, and how building developed from simple longhouses to more sophisticated farmsteads. There are also water mills and wind mills. The Kolu Café serves traditional bean soup and beer. Entrance is free with the Tallinn Card. ⓐ Vabaõhumuuseumi tee 12. ❶ 654 9100. ⓦ www. evm.ee ⓝ Take bus no. 21 or 21b from the train station or minibus 234 from behind the Estonia theatre to Vabaõhumuuseum stop.

● *Pärnu – with its seaside attractions – makes a great place for a break*

Pärnu

Pärnu is Estonia's best-known summer resort. The attraction lies in the shallow sea bay – which becomes warm in June – and the fine, white sandy beaches. The water is clear and unpolluted. Sunbathers started coming here in the 19th century, and they continue to flock here every summer.

Pärnu is a historic Hanseatic harbour town, and also has a university. Besides the nightclubs and other party scenes, Pärnu offers historic sights, museums, conferences, theatre performances and live concerts. Spas and recuperation centres are important here, so most are booked a year in advance, especially in the summer.

GETTING THERE

Pärnu is accessible by car from central Tallinn – take Parnu mnt. (Highway 4) south for 130 km (80 miles). Regular bus services operate between Tallinn and Pärnu, and the journey takes under 2 hours.

Located right in the centre, the Tourist Information Centre provides tips and brochures and has a booth at the beach in summer.

Tourist Information Centre

ⓐ Rüütli 16. ❶ 447 3000. ❶ 447 3001. Ⓦ www.parnu.ee

SIGHTS & ATTRACTIONS

Rüütli tänav

Historic downtown Pärnu is defined by its main pedestrian thoroughfare, Rüütli tänav (Knight Street). The 400 m (440 yd) stretch of the street between Ringi and Vee, and a few streets that branch off from here, are home to a hodge-podge of intriguing

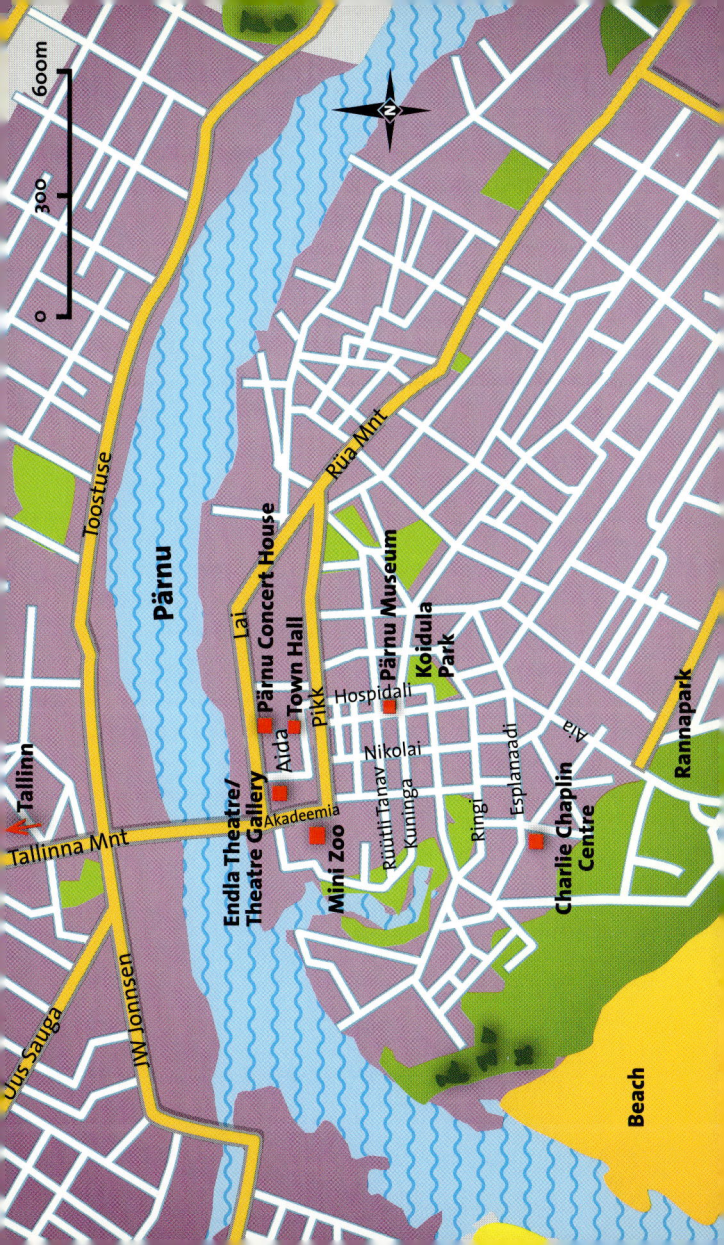

600m

300

0

Toostuse

Pärnu

Rüa Mnt

Tallinn

Tallinna Mnt

Uus-Sauga

JW Jonnsen

**Endla Theatre/
Theatre Gallery**

Akadeemia

Lai

Pärnu Concert House

Aida

Town Hall

Pikk

Hospidali

Pärnu Museum

**Koidula
Park**

Mini Zoo

Ruutli Tanav

Kuninga

Nikolai

Ringi

Esplanaadi

Aia

**Charlie Chaplin
Centre**

Rannapark

Beach

buildings dating from the 17th to the 20th centuries. This is also where you'll find Pärnu's most exclusive shops.

Pärnu Museum

This proudly presents 11,000 years of Pärnu City and County history from the mid-Stone Age to the present. There's even a recreated Soviet-furnished room to remind of the more recent past. Labels are few, but an information sheet should be available.
ⓐ Rüütli 53. ☎ 443 3231. Ⓦ www.pernau.ee. ⏰ Daily 10.00–18.00 (closed Mon–Tues). Admission charge.

Parks

A large part of what makes Pärnu such a relaxing place to visit are its vast, green areas designed for strolling. The most notable of these are Koidula Park, adjacent to the downtown area, with its colourful flowerbeds and fountain, and the Rannapark, established back in 1882, next to the beach. Rannapark is dotted with various sculptures, but the most interesting part is the section west of Mere pst., which is home to some odd works of modern outdoor art, as well as a memorial to the victims of the Estonia ferry disaster of 1994. ⓐ Remmelga 11 Pärnu Eesti. ☎ 503 6564. Ⓦ www.rannapark.ee ⏰ Daily 10.00–22.00 May–Sept.

Mini Zoo

Though the name evokes cute, furry creatures that children would love to pet, the Mini Zoo is in reality a reptile house full of fat pythons and venomous vipers, and even has a pair of confiscated Nile crocodiles. Those furry creatures will be their dinner. Anyone

◆ *The beach is always very busy at the height of summer*

squeamish about reptiles should definitely stay away.
ⓐ Akadeemia 1. ☎ 55 1 6033. ⓦ www.hot.ee/minizoo ⏰ Daily 10.00–18.00; 11.00–16.00 Sat–Sun. Admission charge. 🚌 Trolley 1,2,5; bus 36.

CULTURE

Chaplin Centre (Pärnu New Art Centre)
Originally named after the famous star of silent films, Charlie Chaplin, this cultural centre in a former Communist Party headquarters is a large, cutting-edge venue teeming with activity. To get an idea of the kind of unusual displays you might find here, go around to the back and take a look at the decapitated statue of Lenin, wearing a fibre-glass mock-up of someone else's head. Apart from being home to the Pärnu New Art Museum itself, the centre includes a lobby internet café and foreign language library.
ⓐ Esplanaadi 10. ☎ 443 0772. ⓦ www.chaplin.ee ⏰ Daily 09.00–21.00.

Estonian Lithographic Centre
The workshop for studying lithography, this open studio/art shop is a great place to see at how this form of art is created. ⓐ Kuninga 17. ☎ 55 604 631. ⓦ www.hot.ee/litokeskus ⏰ Daily 12.00–19.00.

Theatre Gallery
The same downtown building that houses the town's largest drama theatre is also home to an art exhibition space. Works are displayed in one large hall, as well as in some of the corridors. ⓐ Keskväljak 1. ☎ 442 0667. ⓦ www.endla.ee ⏰ Daily 14.00–18.00; closed Sun.

Agape Centre/Estonian Methodist Church
The church has an active congregation and a lively cultural centre,

often hosting summer performances. ⓐ Männi 2a. ☎ 445 9888.
🌐 www.agape.parnu.ee 🕐 Daily 11.00–15.00, closed Sat–Sun.

Eliisabeti Church

This historic 18th-century church is also one of Pärnu's favoured
concert venues, and the interior makes it an unforgettable place to
hear music . ⓐ Nikolai 22. ☎ 443 1381.

Endla Theatre

The town's renowned and respected theatre, Endla is a prime venue
for all kinds of cultural happenings. The theatre also houses a
popular café and an art gallery.
ⓐ Keskväljak 1. ☎ 442 0667. 🌐 www.endla.ee

Pärnu Concert Hall

By far the town's largest event venue, this ultra modern structure on
the banks of the river was built in 2002 and has already hosted
many internationally known acts.
ⓐ Aida 4. ☎ 445 5810. 🌐 www.pkm.concert.ee

Pärnu Town Hall (Raekoda)

An elegant setting for classical music, the Town Hall hosts concerts
and other performances for all kinds of festivals throughout the
summer.
ⓐ Nikolai 3. ☎ 443 1325.

RECREATION

Pärnu is where Estonians, especially from Tallinn, come to play and
relax during the long days of summer. So, as you might expect, the

'culture' of the town is more play than theatre. All sorts of recreational opportunities exist from traditional bowling and mini golf to the more adventurous sports of canoeing and hiking. And there's always a day well spent at the amusement park with its twisters and roller coasters.

Bowling
Tervise Paradiis Spa Hotel and Water Park This large recreation complex was opened in 2004 and includes not just bowling but a host of other amenities, including a two-storey water park. ⓐ Side 14, 80010 Pärnu. ❶ 445 1600. ⓦ www.terviseparadiis.ee ❶ 12.00–24.00 Mon–Thur; 12.00–01.00 Fri; 11.00–01.00 Sat; 11.00–24.00 Sun.

Amusement park
Ranna Park For the kid in all of us, this park is filled with all the traditional trappings of a small amusement facility. ⓐ Remmelga 11, Pärnu. ❶ 503 6564. ⓦ www.rannapark.ee ❶ Daily 10.00–22.00 May–Sept.

Bicycle rental
Tõruke
In Rannapark (Beach park), in front of the Mud Bath. ❶ 502 8269. ❶ in Summer: 10.00–20.00 Mon–Sun.

Horse riding
Maria talu Farmstead offering horse riding and other outdoor activities. ⓐ Kõpu küla, Tõstamaa vald, 88109 Pärnumaa. ❶ 447 4558, 523 6066. ⓦ www.maria.ee

◀ *Pärnu's Town Hall is an atmospheric setting for summer events*

Tori Stud Horse riding plus sightseeing trips in horse-drawn wagons at the stables where they breed the good-natured and elegant Tori horse. In winter, wagons are replaced by sledges to get you through the snow. ⓐ Pärn mnt 13, Tori alevik, Tori vald, Pärnu 86801. ⓣ 528 6284. ⓦ www.torihobune.ee

Riisa rantso A touch of western style, for riding lessons and for horse trekking. ⓐ Riisa küla, Tori vald, 86815 Pärnumaa. ⓣ 510 0832 ⓦ www.riisarantso.ee

Canoe trips

Edela Loodusmatkad Gentle canoeing adventures on slow-moving rivers, or a touch of rapids on River Pärnu. ⓐ Pärnade pst 11, Paikuse, 86602 Pärnumaa. ⓣ 445 3188, 50 51 113. ⓦ www.loodusmatkad.ee

Fulvius kanuumatkad A chance to explore and view the scenery from the water. ⓣ 505 3670. ⓦ www.kanuuretked.ee

Hiking

Maria talu Farm (with camping area) has horse riding as well as organised hikes. ⓐ Kõpu küla, Tõstamaa vald, 88109 Pärnumaa. ⓣ 447 4558, 52 36 066. ⓦ www.maria.ee

Tolli talu Another farm, this one on Kihnu island, offering hiking and camping packages. ⓐ Sääre küla, Kihnu saar, 88001 Pärnumaa. ⓣ 446 9908, 52 77 380. ⓦ www.kihnutalu.ee

Golf

Golf courses are just beginning to make an appearance in Estonia, so don't expect too much. Just be happy to spend the day chasing a small white ball over the countryside.

Audru Golf ⓐ Lemmetsa küla, Audru vald, 80041 Pärnumaa. ⓣ 505 9868. ⓦ www.audrugolf.com

Valgeranna Golf ⓐ Valgerand, Audru vald, 88326 Pärnumaa. ❶ 444
3453. Ⓦ www.villaandropoff.fi

Saunas
Pühamüristus ⓐ Saarisoo, Jõesuu, 86802 Pärnumaa. ❶ 506 1896.
Ⓦ www.soomaa.com
Tori kanuumatkad: Põrguwärk Tori, 86801 Pärnumaa. ❶ 511 4253.
Ⓦ www.tori.ee

RETAIL THERAPY

Yasmina Shopping Centre. The most central shopping mall, where
you should find everything you left behind ⓐ Aida 9. For a touch
more individualism in the town's main shopping area, wander
Ruutli Street.

TAKING A BREAK

Chaplin Centre Café € The café in the lobby of the art centre is
probably the most intellectual place in Pärnu to sip tea, and it may
also be the cheapest. ⓐ Esplanaadi 10. ❶ 443 0772.
Ⓦ www.chaplin.ee ❸ Daily 09.00–21.00.

Cibus € Just next to the bus station, this bakery/café provides some
of the freshest cookies and cakes available. ⓐ Ringi 3. ❶ 443 0117.
Ⓦ www.cibus.ee ❸ Daily 07.00–18.00; 07.00–16.00 Sun.

Soorikubaar € A popular place for pastries and especially for
Estonian-style donut rings (sõõrikud). You may have to stand.
ⓐ Pühavaimu 15. ❶ 444 5334. ❸ Daily 07.30–20.00; 09.00–17.00 Sun.

Kadri €–€€ The cheerful, green-coloured Kadri Kohvik is a long-time favourite in downtown Pärnu and holds a special place in the hearts of frequent visitors. Inside you'll find motherly looking ladies serving up traditional Estonian faire at bargain prices. ⓐ Nikolai 12. ⓣ 442 9782. ⓛ Daily 07.30–21.00; 09.00–17.00 Sun.

Lehe €–€€ A sparklingly modern café with hints of a nautical theme in the decor. Locals recommend the food here. ⓐ Lehe 5. ⓣ 442 5788. ⓛ Daily 10.00–24.00.

Jazz Café €€ Soothing music and intriguing artwork make Jazz Café one of Pärnu's most sophisticated places to linger. Watch for live

● *Outdoor cafés are great places to relax and people-watch*

piano performances some evenings. ⓐ Ringi 11. ❶ 442 7546.
ⓦ www.hot.ee/jazzcafe. ❸ Daily 10.00–22.00; Thur–Fri 10.00–24.00;
Sat 09.00–24.00; closed Sun.

AFTER DARK

Brasserie € If you have a big appetite bring it to the buffet
restaurant at the Strand Hotel. Both breakfast and dinner are buffet
style. ⓐ A.H.Tammsaare pst 35, 80010 Pärnu. ❶ 447 5370, 447 5371.
ⓦ www.strand.ee

Kuursaal €–€€ Estonia's biggest tavern, the historic, 1890s-era
Kuursaal near the beach is also a venue for events. A popular stop
for beach-goers looking for just a snack or one of the 'big bellyful'

meals . ⓐ Mere pst. 22. ⓣ 442 0367. Ⓦ www.kuur.ee ⓛ Daily 12.00–18.00; Wed–Thur 12.00–02.00; Fri–Sat 12.00–04.00.

Café Grand €€ When it opened its doors in 1927 the Café attracted the cream of the local society. It reopened in 2001 after extensive renovations and has live music on Fri and Sat nights. ⓐ Kuninga 25, 80010 Pärnu. ⓣ 444 3412/444 341. Ⓦ www.victoriahotel.ee

Lahke Madjar €€ Cheerfully decorated and festooned with strands of garlic, the 'Generous Magyar' offers satisfyingly huge Hungarian dishes in intimate, relaxed surroundings. Nowhere else in town are you likely to find Transylvanian lamb ragout. ⓐ Kuninga 18. ⓣ 444 0104. Ⓦ www.servitris.ee ⓛ Daily 12.00–23.00.

Postipoiss €€ Step inside this cheerful Slavonic kitchen and listen to the music while you try a taste of yet another country. ⓐ Vee 12, 80010 Pärnu. ⓣ 446 4864, 446 4681. Ⓦ www.restaurant.ee

Seegi Maja €€–€€€ The surroundings will make you think you have stepped back into the 17th century. Feast on items that might have graced the plate of Peter the Great. Freshly made, of course. ⓐ Hospidali 1, 80011 Pärnu. ⓣ 443 0555, 443 0556. Ⓦ www.seegimaja.ee

ACCOMMODATION

Konse Holiday Village € Whether you're looking for an actual room or just a place to pitch a tent, this newly built guest house/caravan park on the banks of the river can accommodate. Rooms are sparsely furnished but absolutely spotless, and most have skylights. Showers/WCs are shared. Fifty caravan slots are available, along with all the facilities they need. Management can also arrange boat, jet-ski and bike rental. ⓐ Suur-Jõe 44a. ⓘ 53 435 092. ⓦ www.konse.ee

Aisa Hotel €€ This little hotel, set back from a residential street, has been completely refurbished with modern fixtures and hardwood floors. ⓐ Aisa 39. ⓘ 443 8044. ⓦ www.aisa.ee

Delfine €€ On the street that leads to the beach, Delfine offers stylish rooms with that just-made look. Pop downstairs for a massage or try out the sauna. ⓐ Supeluse 22. ⓘ 442 6900. ⓦ www.delfine.ee

Ene Villa €€ Each of the colourfully painted rooms in this recently built, residential-style guest house has its own outside entrance, WC/shower and satellite TV. Breakfast isn't served, but the owners have thoughtfully provided fridges and coffee makers. ⓐ Auli 10a. ⓘ 442 5532. ⓦ www.hot.ee/villaene.

Freven Villa €€ It may look like just another well-kept historic residence on a quiet Pärnu street, but Freven actually has a little reception desk at the back. Each of the four comfy rooms has its own TV and shower, and every two share a kitchenette, making this a good choice for families. No breakfast. ⓐ Kooli 31. ⓘ 444 1540. ⓦ www.freven.ee

Green Villa €€ This is Green with a capital 'G', as one look at the vibrant exterior paint job will tell you. The historic interior is equally stunning with fireplaces, original hardwood floors and a general early 20th-century feel. Note that 'suites' here are rooms with their own shower and fridge. ⓐ Vee 21. ⓘ 443 6040. ⓦ www.greenvilla.ee

Hommiku Hostel €€ Far too nice to be called a 'hostel', Hommiku resembles a tiny hotel, where each and every room comes with its own shower/WC, TV and even a little kitchen. The location, right in the centre of the Old Town, is hard to beat. No breakfast.
ⓐ Hommiku 17. ☏ 445 1122. Ⓦ www.hot.ee/pav

Jahisadama Guesthouse €€ Ahoy! Every room in the 'Yacht Harbour' Guesthouse is named after a different ship, but you don't have to be an old sea hand to appreciate the brightly coloured decor and great views of the river. Since this is the focal point of Pärnu's

⬤ *Restored to its 1930s glory, the Rannahotell looks shipshape*

sea faring scene, reception can easily arrange boat rental. ⓐ Lootsi 6.
ⓣ 447 1740. ⓦ www.jahisadam.ee

Kanali Puhkemaja €€ This quiet, family-run hotel is virtually hidden
on a residential side street, giving it a peaceful, secluded feel. All
rooms have their own shower and WC. Suites come with their own
small kitchens. Phone ahead when you're arriving to pick up your
keys. ⓐ Kanali 8f. ⓣ 442 5846. ⓦ www.kanali.ee

Koidulapark Hotel €€ A 1905-era hotel overlooking a downtown
park isn't a bad place to spend the night in Pärnu, especially when
its owners have tried to preserve the original style. All the fixtures

and furnishings are new, but some of the wooden flooring dates back to its early days. Prints by classic Estonian artists like Arrak and Wiiralt decorate much of the hotel. Only open April–December.
ⓐ Kuninga 38. ❶ 447 7030. Ⓦ www.koidulaparkhotell.ee

Maritime €€ Completely renovated in 1999, the Maritime is a clean, basic, comfortable hotel close to the beach. ⓐ Seedri 4. ❶ 447 8910. Ⓦ www.pergohotels.ee

Promenaadi €€ A beautiful, painted wooden villa, built in 1905, on a quiet leafy avenue. Rooms here are decorated in a bright, modern style and each comes with cable TV, fridge and its own shower/WC. Free guarded parking at the back. Good location, close to both the city centre and to Ranna Beach. Breakfast not included.
ⓐ Tammsaare pst. 16. ❶ 56 617 623. Ⓦ www.local.ee/promenaadi.

Rahni Guesthouse €€ Close to the centre, 'Woodpecker' Guesthouse not only offers beautifully furnished rooms but a computer and printer in every one! A couple of the larger rooms in the courtyard share a kitchen.
ⓐ Rähni 9. ❶ 443 6222. Ⓦ www.delfine.ee

Sadama Villa €€ As a hotel it may be fairly new, but this villa dates back to 1939. Close to both city centre and the harbour area, with cheery bedrooms and a garden to relax in.
ⓐ Sadama 13. ❶ 447 0008. Ⓦ www.sadamavilla.ee

Alex Maja €€€ Rooms are good-sized and cheerfully decorated. The location, in a little courtyard in the middle of downtown, is a major plus. ⓐ Kuninga 20. ❶ 446 1866. Ⓦ www.alexmaja.ee

Ammende Villa €€€ Far and away the winner in the luxury category is this historic art nouveau mansion surrounded by gardens and fountains. Each of the suites in the 1905-era main house has a personality of its own, and all come furnished with antiques of that period. Classical music performances are held in the garden or the salon each Thursday.
@ Mere pst. 7. ☎ 447 3888. ⓦ www.ammende.ee

Scandic Hotel Rannahotell €€€ Not just another pretty face, the Rannahotell is also an architectural treasure. Dating back to 1937, this striking example of Estonian functionalism has been fully restored and shines in all its original splendour. The hotel makes the most of its beachfront location by offering sea-facing rooms with balconies and an open-terrace bar on the top floor.
@ Ranna pst. 5. ☎ 443 2950. ⓦ www.scandic-hotels.com/rannahotell.

St Peterburg €€€ Bringing a bit of the tsarist 18th century into the heart of Pärnu, the St Peterburg treats its guests to a stylish, old-fashioned ambience. Hallways and rooms here are decorated in the style of the time of Peter the Great, while the older portion of the hotel is reminiscent of Estonia's 17th-century Swedish period. Guests should be sure to check out the hotel's restaurant, wine cellar and sauna. @ Hospidali 6. ☎ 443 0555. ⓦ www.seegimaja.ee

Victoria €€€ Dating back to 1923, the Victoria is a grand old structure with curving walls and lacy windowpanes. Renovation has restored its pre-war elegance, and the classical furnishings in its lobby café keep it on the stylish side. You can hide out with your laptop and do some net surfing – two floors have been outfitted with WiFi. @ Kuninga 25. ☎ 444 3412. ⓦ www.victoriahotel.ee

Tartu

Tartu is the second largest city of Estonia, lying 185 km (116 miles) south of Tallinn. It is known worldwide as a vigorous university town with a rich cultural heritage providing diverse leisure and learning opportunities throughout the year. In addition to Tartu University, founded in 1632, there is the Estonian Agricultural Academy and the Tartu Defence College. Tartu is also known for its research institutions which represent most fields of science.

The Emajõgi River flows through Tartu, adding colour to the city. The first written records of Tartu date from 1030.

GETTING THERE

Some 190 km (120 miles) south-west of Tallinn, Tartu can be reached by car from the capital by following Tartu mnt (Highway 2). Freuquent, regular bus services run between the two cities, with a journey time of 2.5 hours for express services.

Tourist Information Centre in Tartu is a full-service affair, providing travel tips on all of southern Estonia. Here they'll arrange guides, book accommodation and there's an internet terminal.

ⓐ Raekoja plats 14. ❶ 744 2111. Ⓦ www.visittartu.com
🕐 Mon–Fri 09.00–18.00; Sat 10.00–17.00; Sun 10.00–15.00 (mid-May–mid-Sept); Mon–Fri 09.00–17.00; Sat 10.00–15.00; closed Sun (mid-Sept–mid-May)

SIGHTS & ATTRACTIONS

St John's Church (Jaani Kirik)

This magnificent, 14th-century edifice is not only Tartu's oldest

N

Narva Mnt.

Turu Tn.

Riia Tn.

Leaning House

Raekoja Plats

University/Art Museum

Town Hall

KGB Cells

Vabaduse Pst.

Vanemuise

St John's Church

University History Museum

Lai Tn.

Jaani

Toy Museum

Angel's Bridge

Devil's Bridge

Kroonuaia Tn.

Toome Hill

500m

250

Jakobi Tn.

Church of the Virgin Mary

0

surviving church, it's also a treasure trove of medieval sculpture. Its most famous feature is the approximately 1000 terracotta figures that inhabit the church, both inside and out, remnants of some 2000 that it's thought to have had in the Middle Ages. The church was wrecked in World War II and stood derelict for nearly half a century. Now, after 16 years of renovation, it's recently been reconsecrated and is now open to the public.

🅐 Jaani 5. ☎ 744 2229.

Town Hall

The majestic pink building that lords over Town Hall Square is Tartu's Town Hall, built in 1789 by the town's master builder, Rostock-born Johann Heinrich Bartholomäus Walter. It's actually the third town hall to have stood on this spot – the previous two were destroyed by fire. This incarnation mixes early classicism with touches of baroque and rococo. In its day, the cellar and the ground floor on the left side housed a prison, while the right side was a weigh house. Rooms for the Town Council were on the upper floors, and continuing the tradition, the building serves as the city's administrative centre even today. The Town Hall's 18-bell carillon sounds every day at 12.00 and 18.00.

🅐 Raekoja plats.

Leaning House

Estonia's answer to the Leaning Tower of Pisa is the so-called 'Leaning House' at the north-east corner of Town Hall Square. Builders in the 1790s unwisely set part of its foundation on the old city wall and another part on wooden piles. The latter eventually

---

▶ *Not all buildings are on the straight and narrow*

sank, giving the house a noticeable lean. It was in danger of falling over until Polish engineers managed to shore it up during the Soviet period. You can see the inside of the house by visiting the Tartu Art Museum.

Tartu University Main Building

Built in 1809 for the Tartu University's reopening, this grand, neo-classical structure is the symbol of Estonia's biggest brain factory. The building holds three main attractions for visitors: one is the University Art Museum, which displays a collection of classical sculptures, as well as a creepy mummy from the 2nd millennium BC. Sadly, nearly all the sculptures here are plaster copies, as the originals were taken to Russia during World War II.

At the museum, get separate tickets to see the fabulously decorated Assembly Hall (Aula), and the building's most interesting feature, the Student Lock-up. The only one of five such lock-ups that survived a fire in 1965, this is an attic room where, in the 19th century, students were incarcerated for minor offences. The punishment for returning a library book late was two days. Insulting a cloakroom attendant would get you five days, and duelling, three weeks. Cartoons and graffiti still cover the walls.

🕓 Daily 11.00–17.00; closed Sat–Sun. Admission charged for Art Museum, Student Lock-up and Assembly Hall.

Nineteenth-century Tartu Citizen's Home

Providing a fascinating glimpse of what Tartu life was like in the early 19th century, this re-created middle-class dwelling from the 1830s is comprised of a number of rooms, and decorated with the

---

◀ *Did you say seat of learning?*

Biedermeier furniture that was popular in that era. Detailed explanations in English provide a good understanding of the exhibition. Admission 10Kr.

ⓐ Jaani 16. ☏ 736 1545. Ⓦ www.tartu.ee/linnamuuseum.
🕐 Daily 11.00–18.00; closed Mon–Tues.

Tartu City Museum

The best overview of Tartu's history can be found at the City Museum, housed in a beautiful, 18th-century mansion just across the river from Old Town. The collection here isn't terribly extensive, but all the major periods are covered. Don't miss the computer-generated video that shows what medieval Tartu would have looked like.

ⓐ Narva 23. ☏ 746 1911. Ⓦ www.linnamuuseum.tartu.ee
🕐 Daily 11.00–18.00; closed Mon. Admission charge.

University History Museum

Part of the Dome Cathedral is now a museum chronicling the history of Tartu University from its founding in 1632 to the present time. Everything from old lab equipment to student life is presented in this exhibition, which covers a number of floors. The beautiful old library is especially intriguing.

ⓐ Lossi 25. ☏ 737 5677. Ⓦ www.ut.ee 🕐 Daily 11.00–17.00; closed Mon–Tues. Admission charge.

Church of St George the Conqueror

A testament to the exotic beauty of Russian Orthodox architecture, this picturesque pink church just east of the river was originally built in 1870, then reconsecrated in 1945 after postwar restoration. Try to get a peek inside at the elaborate icons.

ⓐ Narva mnt. 103. ☏ 733 3260.

Church of the Virgin Mary

Its full name is actually the Roman Catholic Church of the Immaculate Conception of the Blessed Virgin Mary, but rather than pondering that long label, we suggest coming here for a close-up look at this charming example of late 19th-century, neo-historicist architecture. The church was built in 1899, and features a vaulted interior with stained-glass windows. The altar painting *Virgin Mary with Jesus* dates from 1905.

ⓐ Veski 1a. ☎ 742 2731. 🕐 to visitors Mon–Fri 09.00–11.00 and 17.00–20.00; Sat 09.00–10.00 and 18.00–19.00; Sun 09.00–14.00 Sun (April–Oct). Services Mon, Wed, Fri 17.00; Sat 18.00.

St Paul's Church

Look for this towering church topped with its distinctively square copper spire along Riia, just out of the centre. If the style here looks a bit different from the town's other brick churches, there's good reason – it was built by Finnish architect Eliel Saarinen in 1917. Despite some post-World War II repairs yet to be made, St Paul's is worth a visit for a peek at its bright, art nouveau interior.

ⓐ Riia 27. ☎ 742 0258. 🌐 www.eelk.ee/tartu.pauluse. 🕐 to visitors Mon–Fri 10.00–17.00; Sat 10.00–14.00 ; Sun 09.00–13.00 (April–Sept). Services (in Estonian) 10.00 Sun.

Geology Museum (Geoloogiamuuseum)

If you think this is just another collection of rocks, you're wrong. Though there is a nice collection of minerals in the corridor, most of the display is taken up by hundreds and hundreds of fossils – mainly small marine animals, but also primates and a few mammoth bits from Siberia. May be closed in July. Admission 8Kr.

ⓐ Vanemuise 46. ☎ 737 5839. 🌐 www.ut.ee/BGGM. 🕐 Daily 10.00–16.00; closed Mon–Tues.

Zoology Museum

The University's zoology department keeps a vast collection of stuffed animals – everything from mice to giraffes is on display. If you're not squeamish, check out the 'rat king' – 13 rats who managed to survive with their tails knotted together. This rare find was discovered on a farm in Võru county in early 2005.

ⓐ Vanemuise 46. ☎ 737 5833. 🕐 Daily 10.00–16.00; closed Mon–Tues.

Tartu Toy Museum (Mänguasjamuuseum)

With more toys than even the most shamefully spoiled of children could possibly imagine, this museum could easily keep most youngsters – and probably more than a few adults – wide-eyed for hours. Here you'll see everything from antique paper pop-ups and a 130-year-old doll to an elaborate electric train set that will move if you drop in a 1Kr. coin.

ⓐ Lutsu 8. ☎ 736 1551. ⓦ www.mm.ee 🕐 Daily 11.00–18.00; closed Mon–Tues. Admission charge.

A. le Coq Beer Museum

Mmmm...beer. On the A. Le Coq brewery tour you'll get a glimpse of the mostly automated process by which the company cranks out 40 million litres of beer every year. Most of the tour is spent in the extensive beer museum, set in the old malt drying tower that was still in operation until 1997. The exhibit starts with the beer-making culture of the ancient Sumerians and moves on to show equipment used in this factory since it started up in 1879. Yes, you do get a sample at the end!

ⓐ Tähtvere 56/62. ☎ 744 9711. Tours are held Thur at 14.00 and Sat at 10.00, 12.00 and 14.00. Admission charge.

KGB Cells Museum (KGB Kongid)
As if you needed more reason to dislike the KGB... The KGB Cells
Museum is housed in Tartu's infamous 'Grey House' which was the
regional KGB headquarters in the 1940s and 50s. Apart from the
lock-ups themselves, the museum has extensive exhibits here on
deportations, life in the gulags and Estonian resistance movements.
🅐 Riia 15b (entrance from Pepleri). ☎ 746 1717.
🆆 www.tartu.ee/linnamuuseum 🕐 Daily 11.00–16.00, closed
Sun–Mon. Admission charge.

Toome Hill
Angel's Bridge (Inglisild)
Want to make your dreams come true? Head to Angel's Bridge. It
was built in 1838, and the name is thought to come from a linguistic
twist – part of the hill is landscaped like an English garden and the
words 'English' (Inglise) and 'Angel' (Ingel) are nearly the same in
Estonian. Hold your breath when crossing it and make a wish.

Cathedral Ruins
The massive, red-brick structure at the north-west tip of the hill is the
remains of the Dome Cathedral, which dates from the late 13th century.
It was heavily damaged during the Livonian War and finally finished off
by fire in 1624. It's now home to the University History Museum.

Devil's Bridge (Kuradisild)
Visible from Angel's Bridge, the darker, stone Devil's Bridge is newer,
built in 1913 to honour the 300th anniversary of Romanov rule in
Russia. Like Angel's Bridge, its name might also come from a play on
words – the bridge was built under the supervision of Professor
Mannteuffel, whose name in German translates to 'man-devil'.

Sacrificial stone and Kissing Hill

Pre-Christian Estonians used to worship their pagan gods at the Sacrificial Stone, a large boulder on the north side of the cathedral. This is one of about 400 sacrificial stones scattered around the country where (typically bloodless) sacrifices were made. And the sacrifices continue – nowadays students burn their lecture notes here after exams. Behind the stone is Kissing Hill, where tradition stipulates that newlywed grooms are supposed to carry their brides.

OUTSIDE TARTU

St Peter's Church (Peetri Kirik)

St Peter's is a red-bricked, pseudo-Gothic gem that's definitely worth the short trip over the river to see. It was built in 1884, and features a vast nave wrapped in two levels of galleries, allowing it to seat up to 3000 people. The large altar painting was created by Estonia's seminal artist, Johann Köler, in 1897.

🅐 Narva mnt. 104. ☎ 733 3261. ◑ to visitors June – Aug 10.00–15.00; 09.30–15.00 Sun. Services in Estonian 10.00 Sun.

Tartu Aviation Museum

When you come upon this museum, about 16 km (10 miles) from Tartu, you might get the feeling that some guy has parked a MiG in his backyard. On closer inspection you'll see that the museum is actually more sophisticated than that. The inside of the exhibition house is filled with glass cases containing more than 200 model aircraft, fighters and bombers of every type and manufacture from around the world. It's the outside that most people will be interested in, however. Here there are two helicopters and four fighter jets, including a MiG-21MF and a JA Viggen 37. Visitors can climb ladders to peek into the cockpits. Planes are constantly added to the collection.

ⓐ Veskiorg 1, Lange. ☎ 735 1164. ⓦ www.lennundusmuuseum.ee
🕐 Daily 10.00–18.00. Admission charge

Lahemaa National Park
Lahemaa National Park is a vast area starting just 50 km (31 miles) east of Tallinn, and extending 40 km (25 miles) to Vainupea. The coastline is characterised by four rugged peninsulas, and encompasses sandy beaches, primeval woodland, reed-shrouded coast, peat bogs, well-preserved fishing villages and restored palaces.

The unspoiled natural wilderness is easily accessed by well-marked hiking trails and nature paths. Visitors frequently see roe deer, and occasionally also wild boar and moose. A wide variety of other wild animals inhabit the park. Spring and autumn see migrating flocks of birds.

There is a wide variety of good accommodation and other facilities in the park.

CULTURE

Tartu Song Festival Arena
The most exciting cultural entertainment in Estonia, the song festival, occurs every five years in Tallinn at a place specially built for it. The tradition of Estonian song festivals, which grown from the love of Estonians for choir music, began in 1869. Today there are 30,000 participants and more than 200,000 in the audience.

ⓐ Laulupeo 25, Tartu. ☎ 742 2108. ⓦ www.arena.ee

Vanemuise Concert Hall

Tartu's premiere theatre is housed in this large, downtown facility built in 1967. The same building is home to the Vanemuise Concert Hall. Box office ⏱ Mon–Sat 10.00–19.00, and one hour before performances. ➌ Vanemuise St 6, Tartu. ☎ 737 7530.
Ⓦ www.concert.ee

The Tartu Theatre Laboratory

The Theatre Laboratory experiments with various forms of expression. ➊ Lutsu 2, Tartu. ☎ 746 1045.

Theatre Vanemuine (Big House)

The Theatre Vanemuine, founded in 1870, is the oldest and also the first professional theatre in Estonia. It is the only theatre one whose repertoire includes opera and ballet performances, as well as dramas. The theatre has three different halls: the Big House, the Small House and the Port Theatre.
➊ Vanemuise 6, Tartu. ☎ 744 0165. Ⓦ www.vanemuine.ee

RETAIL THERAPY

Antoniuse Courtyard

If you want to see at first hand how leather goods, pottery, stained glass, woodwork, quilts and other crafts are traditionally made, the Antoniuse Courtyard, across from the Jaani Church, should be your first stop. Members of the Antoniuse Guild, a collective of craftsmen and women, demonstrate their skills to the public. Look for the courtyard to be open by the Hanseatic Days, at the end of June.
➊ Lutsu 5. Ⓦ www.antonius.ee ⏱ 11.00–17.00 Tues–Fri; closed Sat–Mon.

TAKING A BREAK

Bistroo € This old, simple and somewhat stark cafeteria on the square certainly won't win any beauty contests, but it's certainly cheap and handy. ❷ Raekoja plats 9. ☎ 744 3414. ⏰ Daily 07.30–18.00; 09.00–16.00 Sat–Sun.

Kondiitriari € What could be more inviting than the smell of fresh coffee and a huge bakery case packed with pastries? This bakery-café right on Rüütli tänav near the square is understandably a popular destination. If you can, grab a spot on the leather sofa at the back. ❷ Rüütli 5. ☎ 740 0366. 🌐 www.pereleib.ee ⏰ Mon–Fri 08.00–19.00; 09.00–17.00 Sat; 10.00–16.00 Sun.

McDonald's € If you're homesick and absolutely have to have a Big Mac, who is anyone to judge? ❷ Turu 6a. ☎ 734 4346. ⏰ Daily 08.00–24.00; 08.00–02.00 Fri–Sat.

Pagari Pood € Just follow your nose, since this little bakery always seems to be cranking out a large variety of pastries, all ridiculously inexpensive, on a take-away basis. Coffee is a mere 6Kr. ❷ Raekoja plats 2. ⏰ Daily 09.00–20.00; 10.00–18.00 Sat; closed Sun.

Opera Pizza € This plain little café draws a big crowd from the nearby university. That's no shocker since the pizza is actually darned quick and fairly good. Big pizzas for 38–52Kr. ❷ Vanemuise 26. ☎ 742 0795. ⏰ Daily 11.00–21.00; 11.00–22.00 Fri–Sat.

Café Wilde €–€€ The Wilde Pub's ground-floor café is known throughout town for its delectable cakes (try grandma's apple cake), but it's also worth visiting for light meals such as the filled pancakes. More than anything, though, Café Wilde is a place of atmosphere, with its classic, old-fashioned café feel, and with old printing presses in the back paying homage to the two centuries when this building was a publishing house. Drop by in the evenings when it doubles as a wine room. ⓐ Vallikraavi 4. ⓣ 730 97 64. ⓦ www.wilde.ee ⓛ Daily 09.00–20.00; 09.00–22.00 Thur-Sat; 10.00–18.00 Sun.

Crepp €–€€ A touch of France comes to Tartu's Old Town in the form of this classic, old-fashioned Parisian-style café. Naturally it's decorated with black and white photos and has an aloof clientele who are embroiled in conversation about la philosophie and la politique. Crêpes play heavily in the menu (try the one with banana, chocolate and almonds), but you can also find salads, baguettes and quiche. Vive la quiche! ⓐ Rüütli 16. ⓣ 742 2133. ⓦ www.crepp.ee ⓛ Daily 11.00–24.00.

AFTER DARK

Krooks €–€€ Tartu isn't just for intellectuals and academic wannabes; it also, has a place for rockers to gather, and that place is Krooks. In summer the pub is also a stopping place for bikers who travel around the country. It's worth ducking in here, if only to see the weird hodgepodge of beer stickers, medieval armour and other assorted junk that decorates the place. ⓐ Jakobi 34. ⓣ 744 1506. ⓛ Daily 08.00–04.00; 10.00–04.00 Fri–Sat.

ZumZum €–€€ Always an easy stopping place – it's right in the centre of the Old Town – ZumZum attracts a good share of students, foreigners and anyone else interested in watching sports events on the big-screen TV. During the evening it's a cool hangout with pink lights, beads, and black legs in ballet tutus attached to the ceiling. Every so often these sets of legs actually spin around. **ⓐ** Küüni 2. **ⓣ** 744 1438. **ⓦ** www.karsumm.ee **ⓛ** Daily 11.00–24.00; 11.00–01.00 Fri–Sat; 12.00–22.00 Sun.

Big Ben €€ Almost too English with its bright red phone box and portraits of the royals. A vast, two-level affair, Big Ben is roomy enough to accommodate several cricket teams, but it still manages to get mostly full at weekends. If you're feeling posh, head upstairs to the cigar/wine/whisky area and sink into one of its leather wing chairs. The menu at Big Ben naturally includes fish and chips, and it serves around 30 varieties of beer. **ⓐ** Riia 4. **ⓣ** 730 2662. **ⓦ** www.bigbenpub.ee **ⓛ** 07.00–24.00 Mon; 07.00–01.00 Tues–Thur; 07.00–03.00 Fri; 08.00–03.00 Sat; 08.00–24.00 Sun.

Hansa Tall €€ Decked out like an old tavern from Hanseatic times, the Hansa Tall goes all out to create a warm and earthy ambience. **ⓐ** Aleksandri 46. **ⓣ** 737 1802. **ⓦ** www.hansahotell.ee **ⓛ** Daily 10.00–22.00 Sun–Tues; 10.00–24.00 Wed–Thur; 10.00–01.00 Fri–Sat.

Illegaard Jazz Club €€ This cellar is packed as students, intellectuals, and jazz lovers interested in the night's musical performance huddles into this underground space. Don't be surprised to hear brass bands or swing. **ⓐ** Ülokooli 5. **ⓣ** 742 3743. **ⓦ** www.illegaard.ee **ⓛ** Mon–Fri 17.00–02.00; Sat 19.00–02.00; closed Sun.

Õlle Tare €€ Yes, it does look like a giant beer stein, complete with handle. So you won't have to guess what kind of atmosphere you'll find inside. Õlle Tare is essentially a popular, German-style beer hall

that attracts a good mix of young and old. Live bands perform here at weekends, at which time you may have to pay to get in.
ⓐ Aleksandri 42. ① 734 1766. Ⓦ www.olletare.ee Ⓛ Daily 12.00–02.00; 12.00–03.00 Fri–Sat.

Shakespeare €€ One would expect a café in Tartu's Vanemuine Theatre to have a somewhat theatrical air, but Shakespeare goes far beyond the requirement. For a café, this is a large establishment, colourful and comfortable, with framed sketches of Victorian costume designs. More than anything, though, Shakespeare is an

◐ *It's not hard to miss this particular version of the lost island*

evening destination with live piano or guitar performances every night except Sunday. ⓐ Vanemuise 6. ⓣ 744 0140.
ⓦ www.shakespeare.ee ⓛ Daily 10.00–24.00; 10.00–02.00 Fri–Sat.

Ülikooli Kohvik €€ Just north of the town hall square, this café has plenty of seating on two floors (including on a terrace) and live music is on offer. ⓐ Ülikooli 20, Tartu. ⓣ 737 5402. ⓦ www.kohvik.ut.ee ⓛ 1st floor 07.30–19.00 Mon–Fri; 10.00–15.00 Sat; closed Sun. 2nd floor 12.00–01.00 Mon–Thur; 11.00 –01.00 Fri–Sat.

Atlantis €€€ The lost island of Atlantis may still be elusive, but this large restaurant/club complex jutting out over the river is

impossible to miss. With its starched formality and piped classical music, it has the feel of a hotel restaurant without actually being one. Here you can get old standards like chateaubriand and smoked schnitzel, but there's also a 'Kaunas menu' – a tongue-in-cheek nod to Atlantis's Soviet-era name – offering Moscow borscht and vodka snacks. In summer Atlantis clients can also dine on the Pegasus, a boat that will be docked right outside (150Kr). ❸ Narva mnt. 2. ❶ 738 5495. Ⓦ www.atlantis.ee Ⓛ Daily 12.00–24.00; 12.00–01.00 Fri–Sat.

Barclay €€€ For old-fashioned formality and class, the Barclay Hotel's restaurant comes right at the top of the list. Snack on a variety of fresh, buttered bread while waiting for your Elk fillet with game sauce or oven-baked pike perch. Expect professionally-prepared, tasty results and attentive service. ❸ Ülikooli 8. ❶ 744 7100. Ⓦ www.barclay.ee Ⓛ Daily 12.00–22.00; closed Sun.

Pussirohu Kelder €€€ If you're a newcomer to Tartu, this place is a must. The Gunpowder Cellar is an amazing place, literally built into a vast, brick gunpowder vault that was carved into a downtown hillside in the mid-18th century. If you're hungry, try the soup served in a bread bowl or the dangerous garlic bread dish called 'kiss me more'. The cellar tends to fill up when live bands hit the stage (you may have to pay admission). ❸ Lossi 28. ❶ 730 3555. Ⓦ www.pyss.ee Ⓛ Daily 12.00–02.00; 12.00–03.00 Fri–Sat.

Werner €€€ Most Tartu residents know about the Werner café, but the same establishment also runs a fully-fledged restaurant upstairs. With its more formal setting and cognac room, it's a world away from the grandmothers and students munching on pastries downstairs. ❸ Ülikooli 11. ❶ 744 1274. Ⓛ Daily 12.00–23.00; 12.00–20.00 Sun.

ACCOMMODATION

Hostel (Tartu Student Village) € The dorms are much nicer than that you'd ever expect for a student residence. For location, quality and price, they're probably the best deals in town. Narva mnt. 27. 740 9955. www.kyla.ee

Hostel Pepleri (Tartu Student Village) € The biggest of the three Student Village options, each room has its own kitchen, bathroom, TV and internet connection. There's also a sauna and laundry facility in the building. Breakfast isn't provided, but the downtown location is a big plus. Pepleri 14. 740 9955. www.kyla.ee

Starest € Renovated in 2004, Starest has unbelievably spiffy rooms for the price. All are brightly decorated and have wood floors and satellite TV. The drawback is the distant location, in the Annelinn suburb. Take bus no.1 or 3A to the Mõisavahe stop. Mõisavahe 21. 740 0674. www.starest.ee

Tartu € In addition to its more standard, higher-priced rooms, the Tartu also offers 'youth rooms' aimed at the backpacker set. These are all fairly basic triple rooms with TVs. Showers/WCs are in the corridor. The location near the bus station is a plus. Breakfast is extra. Soola 3. 731 4300. www.tartuhotell.ee

Era Villa €€ This pretty art nouveau villa was recently renovated to its original 1914 look. The public rooms retain some period features. Ten minutes' walk from the centre of town, the rooms are clean, comfortable with all the usual facilities and decorated with some modern touches. Era 1. 731 4380. www.eravilla.ee

Park €€ True to its name, this hotel sits in a downtown park, just a short walk from all the major sights. Opened in 1940, it's not the newest of hotels, and has the creaky floors to prove it. There's a distinct air of timelessness here – management still proudly talk about the Kekkonen suite, where that Finnish president stayed, albeit very briefly, in the 1960s. Rooms vary, but come fully equipped. Ⓐ Vallikraavi 23. ❶ 742 7000. Ⓦ www.parkhotell.ee

Uppsala Maja €€ This is an enchanting, 250-year-old building – one of Tartu's oldest wooden structures – which provides cosy rooms in the style of an early 20th-century Swedish town house. You might have seen some of the furniture before – it all comes from Ikea, in keeping with the link to Uppsala, Sweden. Every couple of rooms share a bath. There's a roomy kitchen and a little patio for outdoor dining. Ⓐ Jaani 7. ❶ 736 1535. Ⓦ www.uppsalamaja.ee

Vikerkaare €€ is an unexpected find – a small but respectable guest house on a residential street in the Tähtvere district, just outside the centre. The rooms have TVs and own shower/WC. Ⓐ Vikerkaare 40. ❶ 742 1190. Ⓦ www.hot.ee/tdc

Draakon €€€ You won't find a more central location than this – the Draakon is right on Town Hall Square, next to the Kissing Students fountain. At the same time, its interior is somehow serene, with hints of old-fashioned elegance and biggish rooms. Ⓐ Raekoja plats 2. ❶ 744 2045. Ⓦ www.draakon.ee

Hansa Hotell €€€ Big, colourful and cosy rooms, some decorated with striped wallpaper, others with brick, set Hansa apart from its rivals. Some suites even have little bar areas. The real difference at

Hansa, though, is the complex's Hanseatic-style courtyard, a wide, outdoor tavern with wooden wagons, a windmill and other props. The indoor part of the tavern is equally theatrical, and even has a smoke sauna. ⓐ Aleksandri 46. ⓣ 737 1800. ⓦ www.hansahotell.ee

London €€€ A touch of class in the Old Town – there's even a fountain in the lobby! Rooms are modern and plush, nicely decorated in striking colours, and some have interesting views of the surrounding old streets and rooftops. ⓐ Rüütli 9. ⓣ 730 5555. ⓦ www.londonhotel.ee

Pallas €€€€ The only risk in choosing Pallas is that you might not want to leave your room. This spiffy hotel on the upper floors of a downtown business/shopping centre has great views both inside and out. From its windows you can easily spy on the crowds moving into the Old Town. Much more fascinating is the interior – in homage to the Pallas art school that operated in the early part of the 20th century, all the rooms are decorated with at least one wall of painting, while suites are transformed into amazing, modern art canvases that have to be seen to be believed. Check out the photos on their website. ⓐ Riia mnt. 4. ⓣ 730 1200. ⓦ www.pallas.ee

ⴰ *Choose a central location if you wish*

Spas outside Tallinn

If you want to extend your city break to Tallinn and fancy a few days' relaxation or the chance to try indulgent beauty treatments, then why not head to a spa? Or you may think your health would benefit from professional treatment, medicine that will go down all the better when it also offers the chance to explore a little more of Estonia and the benefits of sea air. Tallinn has several spa hotels (see pages 14–15), but there are also a number of impressive spas dotted around the country.

On offer are a range of programmes from pampering beauty treatments and massages to more invasive procedures – so do check these are appropriate with your own doctor before you travel.

The cost of your stay will depend on the treatments you opt for – check the spa's website for details of spa packages it offers.

SPAS IN ESTONIA

Haapsalu

Fra Mare Spa Tucked into tiny little Haapsalu, about 100 km (60 miles) from Tallinn, is this 200-year-old health resort. The powers of its healing mud have been known since 1812. Not to worry, the buildings are all quite modern and the treatments are up-to-the-minute. The hotel has 72 rooms, restaurant, seawater swimming pool, sauna and a gym. As well as traditional beauty treatments, services include: aroma massage, acupressure, cellulite massage, chocolate body wrap, electrotherapy, ear candling, traditional massage, reiki, salt chambers and red grape body wrap.
🅐 Ranna tee 2, Haapsalu. ☎ 472 4600. 🌐 www.framare.ee

Pärnu

Estonia Spa This supersize complex seems to be forever expanding, and Housed in three buildings, with the White House and the Green House connected by an elevated glass walkway. the famous Pärnu Mudaravila, that beautiful, domed building near the beach. Each facility offers decent, hotel-style rooms and a full range of treatment options. Most guests arrive in large groups and convalesce here for a week, so it's best to book at least a month in advance. 🅐 Tammsaare tee 4a, Pärnu. ☎ 447 9905. 🖶 447 6901. 🌐 www.spaestonia.ee

Sõprus Health Rehabilitation Centre Some guests prefer to stay in the spa's classic yellow wooden villa, but, most are housed in the more modern adjacent building attached to the treatment centre. Rooms are all fully outfitted, some have balconies, and most have internet connections. 🅐 Eha 2, Pärnu. ☎ 445 0750. 🖶 445 0770.
🌐 www.spahotelsoprus.com

Tervise Paradiis The largest spa hotel in Estonia – and indeed the Baltics – is just 1 km (0.6 miles) from the beach. Its seven buildings are connected by glass galleries, giving them a decidedly space-age look. A full range of therapies is available and rooms here rival those in Pärnu's best hotels. ❸ Side 14. ❶ 445 1606. Ⓦ www.terviseparadiis.ee

Viiking Hotel and Health Rehabilitation Centre This attractive, modern sanatorium near the yacht harbour is also a fine hotel, a few steps ahead of others in town in terms of comfort. Healthy services run the whole gamut, from infra-red sauna to honey massage. This is also one of Estonia's leading cardiac treatment centres, so don't worry about over-exerting yourself during your stay. ❸ Sadama 15, Pärnu. ❶ 443 1293. Ⓦ www.viiking.ee

Villa Medica Pärnu's smallest sanatorium is in fact a private clinic specialising in treatment of musculoskeletal problems, but it makes its hotel rooms available to both patients and non-patients alike. Day surgery, beauty treatments and massage are also available. ❸ Tammsaare 39. ❶ 442 7121. ❶ 442 7121.

Eastern Estonia
Saka Cliff Hotel and Spa The neo-Renaissance Saka Manor, which dates from the 19th century and is being renovated into the North Estonian Visitor Centre, and the park surrounding it are situated on the limestone bank of northern Estonia, where the 1200 km (750 mile) Baltic Klint reaches its highest point.

Spa services include a range of massage treatments and both infrared and steam sauna.
❸ Kohtla vald, Ida-Virumaa, about 160 km (100 miles) from Tallinn along the St Petersburg road. ❶ 343 0764. Ⓦ www.saka.ee

Toila Sanatorium Like many other Estonian sanatoriums, this sanatorium specialises in treating chronic problems with muscles, joints and spine and cardiovascular diseases. What sets the Toila apart from other places is the salt chamber, used for treatment of all chronic diseases of respiratory organs.

Other services include: 'electric sleep', which has a stabilizing effect on the nervous system; curative baths; and thermal paraffin and ozocerite treatments for traumatic injuries and inflammations of joints and muscles. ② Ranna 12, Toila. ☎ 334 2900. ⓦ www.toilasanatoorium.ee

Laulasmaa Spa

The resort's health centre offers different types of massage (body massage, aroma massage, underwater massage and Thai massage), electric and laser therapy, ozocerite therapy, salt therapy, aromatherapy, water therapy (including pearl and herb baths) and solarium.

⬤ Typical spa architecture and style. This one is Pärnu's Estonia Spa

The spa also offers a water park with a variety of water attractions to cater for all ages, such as 20 m (22 yd) swimming pool, outdoor pool, counter-current pool, children's pool, whirlpool, waterfall, massage pool, Finnish sauna, infrared sauna, steam saunas and solarium.

ⓐ Puhkekodu 4, Harjumaa. ❶ 687 0800. ❻ 687 0801.
ⓦ www.laulasmaa.ee

Kalvi Manor A truly majestic seaside manor lovingly restored by Danish and Estonian owners. Among the lordly pursuits offered on this 2000 hectare (5000 acre) estate are hunting and skeet shooting. There's an indoor pool, winter garden and saunas, too. The 19th-century Kalvi is said to be the only manor house in Estonia built in English style and it's certainly got that feel. ⓐ Near the village of Aseri, 100 km (60 miles) east of Tallinn. ❶ 339 5300.
ⓦ www.kalvi-hotel.com

Muhu Island

Pädaste Manor This place is almost too good to be true! – a 15th-century island manor transformed into a top-notch hotel. Word of this classy getaway has already spread far and wide, attracting foreign presidents and rock stars. While it's luxurious, it's not staid; the facilities include a private movie theatre, a helipad, a Muhu smoke sauna and nearby horse riding. Their restaurant, SeaHouse, is also top-notch – comparable to the very best in Tallinn. Ask to see the old Soviet missile silos not far from Pädaste. ⓐ On Muhu Island, just 10 minutes from where the ferry docks. ❶ 454 8800. ❻ 454 8811.
ⓦ www.padaste.com

---

❶ *If you need to surf, there is no shortage of internet cafés*

Directory

GETTING THERE

By air

The easiest way to get to Tallinn is to fly. Tallinn International Airport is fully modern and user friendly. It is serviced by direct flights from 23 cities in Europe, including London (Gatwick), Manchester and Dublin via Estonia Air. Easyjet flies to Tallin from London Stansted. The airport has a full range of services, including currency exchange, banks and ATMs, and it is wise to have some local currency before starting into town.

By car

Driving across Europe to Tallinn can take a long time, with the total distance from Calais being about 2460 km (1540 miles). The roads are good and fast through Western Europe, but once you reach Poland the pace will slow, as there are few multi-lane fast highways in Poland and the Baltic States.

By rail

There is a direct service to the Russian cities of Moscow and St Petersburg, and to the rest of Europe via Latvia. In general, railway systems throughout the Baltic States are poor. The *Thomas Cook European Rail Timetable* has up-to-date schedules for European international and national train services.

Thomas Cook European Rail Timetable ❶ (UK) 01733 416477; (USA) 1 800 322 3834. ⓦ www.thomascookpublishing.com

By bus

There is a regular bus service to Riga in Latvia and Vilnius, Lithuania, with connections to most other major European cities through Eurolines (Ⓦ www.eurolines.com) and Ecolines (Ⓦ www.ecolines.ee) who run services to Tallinn from a number of cities in Germany and eastern Europe.

By ferry

The Tallinn Passenger Port is located about 1 km (0.6 miles) north-east of the city centre. There are regular ferry and catamaran connections from Helsinki, operated mainly by Tallink, Silja Line and Nordic Jet Line, and a ferry service from Stockholm run by Tallink.
Port of Tallinn ☎ 372 631 8550 Ⓦ www.ts.ee

ENTRY FORMALITIES

Documentation

A valid passport is required to enter the country. Since Estonia joined the EU in 2004, entry into the country for most people has become very easy. Entry from another EU country is normally very quick, although entry from Russia can take some time. Citizens of most countries do not require a visa unless they plan to stay longer than 90 days. Children aged 7 to 15 years must have their own passport when travelling to Estonia unless they are registered in a parent's passport, in which case there should be a photo of the child next to the name. Children under 7 years do not require a photo if they are registered in a parent passport.

For more information or to check the visa status of your country, check the website of the Estonian Ministry of Foreign Affairs Ⓦ www.vm.ee/eng.

Customs

There are some restrictions on the import of dairy products and milk. The import of tobacco products, alcohol and prescription medicines is allowed, but the amount is limited. Customs information for Estonia is available at Ⓦ www.cutoms.ee.

🔽 *Ferries link Tallinn to Helsinki if you fancy heading to Finland*

MONEY

The national currency is the Estonian kroon (Kr.). One kroon equals approximately 0.06 euros. The kroon is broken down into 100 sents. There are coins of 5, 10, 20 and 50 sents, and of 1 and 5Kr. There are banknotes of 1, 2, 5, 10, 22, 50, 100 and 500Kr.

Traveller's cheques can be exchanged in banks, but are less likely to be accepted in shops. Eurocheque is the most widely accepted traveller's cheque, but American Express and Thomas Cook are also accepted. Most larger hotels, stores and restaurants accept Visa, MasterCard, Eurocard, Diner's Club and American Express. Many shops and restaurants, especially those frequented by tourists, will accept euros. However, it is always advisable to carry some Estonian kroons with you.

Banks and ATMs are plentiful and easy to find in Tallinn. Banks are normally open 09.00–18.00 on weekdays, while some offices are also open on Saturday mornings. All banks offer currency exchange. Exchange offices are also found in larger hotels, the airport, train station, ferry terminal, and major shopping centres.

HEALTH, SAFETY & CRIME

Estonia is relatively safe in terms of health problems. No immunisations or health certificates are required before visiting. If you plan to hike in wooded or boggy areas, you should be vaccinated against tick-borne encephalitis. The tap water is safe to drink, although it may be less than palatable.

Minor ailments can usually be treated at pharmacies, which carry a wide range of international drugs from painkillers to antibiotics. Pharmacies are normally open from 10.00 to 19.00, but one, Linnaapteek, is open 24 hours a day. It is located in the city centre: ❸ Pärnu Maantee 10. ❶ 644 2262.

Major complaints are best treated at a hospital (*haigla*). Emergency treatment is free, but if you are admitted to hospital, you will be charged a fee for bed space and drugs.

The standard of medical care is high, and most doctors speak some English. There are private clinics with English-speaking doctors in Tallinn. EU health-care privileges apply in Estonia, so travellers from the UK require a European Health Insurance Card (EHIC). However, this only guarantees emergency treatment, not all possible expenses, so you should have good health insurance when visiting Tallinn. See Emergencies, page 156, for details of local clinics.

Estonia has a relatively low crime rate. However, tourist attractions, such as the Old Town, are prime hunting grounds for sneak thieves, muggers and pickpockets. Keep expensive mobile phones and camera equipment out of sight as much as possible, and leave expensive jewellery at home. If you have a car, park it in a guarded, well-lit car-park. You should not walk the streets alone after dark.

If you are the victim of crime, be patient with the police. Many officers, especially the older ones, are not fluent in English. The police are generally courteous and businesslike, but can be slow in filling out crime report forms.

Visitors are required to carry identification at all times, although it is unlikely that you will be required to produce it except when entering and leaving the country.

OPENING HOURS

Shops Generally open 10.00–19.00 Mon–Fri, with early closing on Saturday. Some may open on Sundays in the main tourist areas.
Banks 09.00–18.00 Mon–Fri.

Museum opening hours vary, with longer opening hours between May and September.

TOILETS

A triangle pointing down indicates the men's room (or an M or *Meeste*) and a triangle pointing upward is the women's room. The most central public toilets are to be found in the Old Town. Disabled facilities are available in Town Hall Square. The city also has several Swedish-built automatic WC facilities which require two 1Kr coins.

CHILDREN

Tallinn, especially the Old Town, can be quite a child-friendly place. Locals love to take their children to the zoo, puppet shows and the cinema, and to see the swans in the lake by Kadriorg. Your little one won't lack for new experiences.

Children are also quite welcome at some of the more serious places such as concert halls. However, it might be best to select balcony seats in case you need to make a quick getaway at any point.

- **Transport** Children under the age of 3 ride for free on Tallinn's public transport system. Need a taxi large enough to accommodate a pram or pushchair? Advise the dispatcher and you'll be sent a car large enough to suit your needs.

- **Dining** Most restaurants and cafés happily serve children, and some even have a special menu available. Estonians are so tolerant of children you may discover the chef is quite willing to make something special to appease a little appetite.

- **Quick Change Necessary?** Most department stores such as Stockmann and Kaubamaja have nappy-changing facilities.

- **Medical** First aid is available at the Tallinn Children's Hospital.
  ⓐ 28 Tervise. ☎ 697 4146 or 697 4194 (Trauma).

- **Old Town** Daydreams of knights in shining armour and great battles fought to capture the castle are almost guaranteed during a walk through this medieval bastion. With luck you'll find knights, damsels and jesters wandering the streets.

- **Estonian Puppet Theatre** Suitable for children of all ages!
  ⓐ Pärnu mnt 5. ☎ 667 9555. 🕐 10.00–18.00.

- **Tallinn Zoo** Established in 1939, the zoo is home to over 5000 animals representing nearly 350 species. Children will love the petting zoo filled with rabbits, hamsters and other small, child-friendly animals. ⓐ Paldiski mnt 145. ☎ 694 3300.
  🅦 www.tallinnzoo.ee ⓝ From the city centre take trolley no. 6 or bus no. 22 to Zoo stop. 🕐 Daily 09.00–17.00; indoor exhibitions closed Mon.

- **Tallinn Science and Technology Centre** Oodles of interactive exhibits, computer classes and lightning demonstrations.
  ⓐ Pohja pst 29. ☎ 715 2650. 🅦 www.energiaskeskus.ee
  🕐 Mon–Fri 10.00–17.00; Sat 12.00–17.00. Admission charged, free with Tallinn card.

COMMUNICATIONS
Phones
The telephone system in Estonia is reliable and easy to use. All numbers within the country have seven digits and there are no area codes. Tallinn has a good supply of public telephone boxes, but they

use magnetic cards and not coins. The public phones offer international direct dialling, and many have English-language instructions posted inside. If you will be making calls from pay phones, you can purchase cards in denominations of 30, 50 and 100Kr. These are available from post offices, newspaper and tobacco kiosks, some supermarkets and the tourist information office.

Calling into and out of Estonia is easy. To call in, simply dial your country's international access code, then 372 (Estonia's country code) and then the seven digit number. To call out dial 00, then the country code and then the local number.

If you have a GSM mobile phone, it is possible to avoid heavy roaming charges by purchasing a prepaid SIM card from one of the local services, such as EMT Simpel or Tele2 Smart. Starter packs and refills are available at newspaper kiosks.

Post

The Estonia postal system is very efficient. The Tallinn Central Post Office is conveniently located at Narva Maantee 1, near the centre of the city. There are also post offices in other parts of the city. Many post offices have some staff that speak English.

The Central Post Office is open 07.30 to 20.00 weekdays, 09.00 to 18.00 Saturday, and 09.00 to 15.00 Sunday. Normal hours of operation for other post offices are 09.00 to 18.00 weekdays, and 9.00 to 15.00 Saturday.

The cost of sending a letter to the rest of Europe is 6.5Kr, and to North America and Australia it is 8Kr.

Beside normal postal services, post offices can also be used to send and receive faxes, and to use the internet.

Information on postal services is available at ☏ 661 6616 and at ⓦ www.tallpost.ee.

Faxes can be sent and received from several locations:

Tallinn Central Post Office ⓐ Narva mnt. 1. ❶ 625 7300.

Olümpia Hotel's Business Centre ⓐ Liivalaia 33. ❶ 631 5333.

Hotel Radisson SAS Tallinn ⓐ Rävala pst. 3. ❶ 669 0000.

● *Cards – phone and postal – are readily available in the city*

Internet

Tallinn is well served by internet cafés, which is not surprising given the high level of use by its citizens. The cost is 40–60Kr for an hour. Internet access is also available in public libraries, but there can be a waiting time to get on a terminal.

Public access to the internet is offered in the following locations:

@5 Tallinna 🄰 Kaubamaja Gonsiori 2.

Apollo 🄰 Raamatumaja Viru 23.

Balti Sepik 🄰 Süda 1.

Café Espresso 🄰 Estonia pst. 7.

Café Sookoll 🄰 Soo 42.

Central Library 🄰 Estonia pst. 8.

Central Post Office 🄰 Narva maantee 1.

Demini Department Store 🄰 Corner of Viru and Vene Str.

Mustamäe Shopping Centre 🄰 Tammsaare tee 116.

Pitstop 🄰 Mündi 2.

Stockmann Department Store 🄰 Liivalaia 53.

WW Passaazh 🄰 Aia 3.

For a small charge, internet access is readily available at the following cafés and locations:

Demini Khovik 🄰 Viru 1/Vene 2. ☎ 5622 9922. 🕐 Daily 08.00–19.00; 08.00–17.00 Sun.

Estonian National Library internet hall Free if booked in advance. 🄰 Tõnismägi 2 (room C-2118). ☎ 630 7381. 🌐 www.nlib.ee 🕐 Tues, Wed and Fri 12.00–1900; Mon and Thur 10.00–17.00 Thur; closed Sat–Sun.

Kaubamaja internet centre 🄰 Gonsiori 2, Tallinna Kaubamaja 5th floor. ☎ 667 3100. 🕐 Daily 09.00–21.00.

Neo 🄰 Väike-Karja 12. ☎ 628 2333. 🕐 Daily 10.00–23.00.

Pitstop 🄰 Mündi 2a. ☎ 641 8154. 🌐 www.pitstopbar.ee 🕐 Mon–Tues

14.00–24.00; Wed–Thur 14.00–01.00; Fri–Sat 14.00–03.00.
Reval Café ❷ Aia 3. ☎ 627 1229. Ⓦ www.revalcafe.ee
🕔 Daily 10.00–23.00.

ELECTRICITY

The electrical system in Estonia is very reliable. It is 220 volts AC, 50
hertz. The plug is two pin, European style.

TRAVELLERS WITH DISABILITIES

The Baltic States have a long way to go to become truly wheelchair-
accessible, or even friendly. Even in the larger cities access to public
transport and tourist attractions is sadly lacking. The spa resorts
have been catering to those with disabilities since the mid-19th
century and it is in these areas you will find hotels and restaurants
that are better acquainted with physically challenged travellers.

Tourist offices can be especially helpful in determining if there is
suitable accommodation in the area you wish to visit if you make
your request in advance. It's a good idea to double-check any
information you receive, since some establishments will advertise
services that are still to be implemented.

If you travel with a wheelchair, have it serviced before your
departure and carry any essentials you may need to do repairs.
It is also a good idea to travel with any spares of special clothing or
equipment that might be difficult to replace.

Associations dealing with your particular disability can be
excellent sources of information on conditions and circumstances
in other countries. The following contacts may be helpful:

United Kingdom and Ireland

Tripscope ❷ Alexandra House, Albany Road, Brentford, Middlesex,

TW8 ONE. ☎ 0845/758 5641. Ⓦ www.tripscope.org.uk.
Irish Wheelchair Association ⓐ Blackheath Drive, Clontarf. Dublin 3.
☎ 01/818 6400. Ⓦ www.iwa.ie.

USA and Canada
Society for the Advancement of Travelers with Handicaps (SATH)ⓐ
347 5th Avenue. New York, NY 10016. ☎ 212/447-7284. Ⓦ
www.sath.org.
Access-able Ⓦ www.access-able.com

Australia and New Zealand
Australian Council for Rehabilitation of the Disabled (ACROD) ⓐ PO
Box 60. Curtin ACT 2605. Suite 103, 1st Floor, 1-5 Commercial Road.
Kings Grove 2208. ☎ 02/6282 4333. Ⓦ www.acrod.org.au.
Disabled Persons Assembly ⓐ 4/173-175 Victoria Street. Wellington.
☎ 04/801 9100. Ⓦ www.dpa.org.nz.

FURTHER INFORMATION

Tallinn City Tourist Office Ⓦ www.tourism.tallinn.ee
Estonian Tourist Board Ⓦ www.visitestonia.com
Pärnu Tourist Board Ⓦ www.parnu.ee
Tartu Tourist Office Ⓦ www.tartu.ee

Useful phrases

Although English is spoken in Tallinn, these words and phrases may
come in handy. See also the phrases for specific situations in other
parts of the book.

English	Estonian	Approx. pronunciation
BASICS		
Yes	Jah (jaa)	Yah (ya-a)
No	Ei	Nine
Please	Palun	Pah-loon
Thank you	Tänan (Aitäh)	Ta-nan (Ay-tahh)
Hello	Tere, tervist	Teh-reh/ter-vis
Goodbye	Nägemiseni (head aega)	Na-ghe-mi-seh-ni(he-a-da-e-ga)
Excuse me	Vabandage	Vah-ban-da-gheh
Sorry	Andke andeks	And-keh and-eks
That's okay	See sobib	See sobib
I don't speak Estonian	Ma ei oska eesti keelt	Mah ey os-kah e-es-ti ke-elt
Do you speak English?	Kas te räägite/ oskate inglise keelt?	Kas te rae-aeghi-te/ os-ka-te ing-li-seh ke-elt?
Good morning	Tere hommikut	Teh-reh hom-mi-kuht
Good afternoon	Tere päevast	Teh-reh pa-vahst
Good evening	Tere õhtust	Teh-reh oh-tuhst
Goodnight	Head ööd	He-ad urd
My name is ...	Minu nimi on...	Minu nimi on...

	DAYS & TIMES	
Monday	Esmaspäev	Es-mas-pa-ev
Tuesday	Teisipäev	Tey-si-pa-ev
Wednesday	Kolmapäev	Kol-mah-pa-ev
Thursday	Neljapäev	Nel-ya-pa-ev
Friday	Reede	Re-e-deh
Saturday	Laupäev	Lau-pa-ev
Sunday	Pühapäev	Puh-ha-pa-ev
Morning	Hommik	Hom-mik
Afternoon	Päev	Pa-ev
Evening	Ohtu	Oh-tuh
Night	Öö	Ur
Yesterday	Eile	Ey-leh

English	Estonian	Approx. pronunciation
Today	Tana	Tanah
Tomorrow	Homme	Hom-meh
What time is it?	Mis kell on?	Mis kell on?
It is …	Kell on …	Kell on …
09.00	Täpselt üheksa	Tap-selt yuh-hek-sah
Midday	Keskpäev	Kesk-pa-ev
Midnight	Kesköö	Kesk-o-o

NUMBERS

One	Üks	Yuks
Two	Kaks	Kaks
Three	Kolm	Kolm
Four	Neli	Neli
Five	Viis	Vees
Six	Kuus	Coos
Seven	Seitse	Seyt-seh
Eight	Kaheksa	Kah-hek-sah
Nine	Üheksa	Yu-hek-sah
Ten	Kümme	Kym-meh
Eleven	Üksteist	Yuks teyst
Twelve	Kaksteist	Kaks-teyst
Twenty	Kakskümmend üks	Kah-hek-sah-teys
Fifty	Viiskümmend	Vees-kyum-mend
One hundred	Sada	Sah-da

MONEY

I would like to change these traveller's cheques/this currency	Ma tahaksin vahetada need reisitsekid/ selle valuuta	Mah tah-hak-sin vah-heh-ta-da ne-ed rey-si-tseh-kid/ sel-leh vah-lootah
Where is the nearest ATM?	Kus on lähim sularahaautomaat?	Kus on lahim sularahah-owtomaht?
Do you accept credit cards?	Kas te võtate vastu krediitkaarte?	Kas te vyuitate vastu kred-di-it-kar-ar-te?

SIGNS & NOTICES

Airport	Lennujaam	Len-nuh-jahm
Rail station/Platform	Raudteejaam/Platvorm	Rowd-te-eh-ya-am/Plat-form
Smoking	Suitsetajatele	Suyt-seh-tah-yah-the-leh
Non-smoking	Mittesuitsetajatele	Mit-teh-suyt-seh-tah-yah-the-leh
Toilets	WC (Tualettruum)	Veh-tseh (Tu-a-lett-room)
Ladies/Gentlemen	Naistele/Meestele	Nays-the-leh/me-es-teh-leh

Emergencies

EMERGENCY NUMBERS
The following are all national free emergency numbers:
Fire ☎ 112
Police ☎ 110
Ambulance ☎ 112

The Estonian police force (*politsei*) was established in 1991. Officers wear dark blue uniforms, and have special uniforms for festive occasions.

MEDICAL SERVICES
For entry into Estonia, it is advisable (but not mandatory) to have a valid health insurance policy. No vaccinations or health certificates are required. In case of accident or serious illness, ☎ 112.

Pharmacies (*Apteek*) are usually open from 10.00–19.00, but one stays open all night (🅰 Linnaapteek, Pärnu mnt 10. ☎ 644 2262). Ordinary medication is available in all pharmacies.

CONSULATES & EMBASSIES
Australia Consulate 🅐 c/o Standard Ltd, Marja 9, Tallinn.
☎ 650 9308.
Canada Embassy 🅐 Toom-kooli 13, 10130 Tallinn. ☎ 627 3311.
Republic of Ireland Embassy 🅐 Vene 2, 10123 Tallinn. ☎ 681 1888.
South Africa Representation 🅐 Rahapajankatu 1 A 5 00160, Helsinki, Finland. 🆆 www.southafricanembassy.fi
UK Embassy 🅐 Wismari 6, 10136 Tallinn. ☎ 667 4700.
USA Embassy 🅐 Kentmanni 20, 15099 Tallinn. ☎ 668 81 00.

🔽 *Estonia's finest on patrol in the Old Town*

EMERGENCY PHRASES

Help! Appi! *Ap-pi!*   **Fire!** Põleb! *Poleb!*   **Stop!** Stopp! *Stop!*

Call an ambulance/a doctor/the police/the fire service!
Kutsuge kiirabi/arst/politsei/tuletõrje!
Kyut-su-keh keer-ah-bi/arst/po-lit-sey/tu-leh-tor-ye!

The publishers would like to thank the following individuals and organisations for supplying their copyright photographs for this book.
A1 Pix: pages 15, 17, 33, 35, 39, 41, 51, 87, 95, 99, 102, 106, 110, 117, 130, 139, 141, 144 and 157.
Ann Carroll Burgess: 1, 26, 77 and 150.
Tom Burgess: 5 and 67.
Tallinn Tourism: 7, 9, 13, 42, 49, 63, 69 and 85 (Toomas Volmer); 21, 23, 73 and 91 (Tavi Grepp); 29, and 93 (Kaido Haagen).
Tartu.ee/Meelis Lokk: 135 and 118

Proofreader: Janet McCann
Copy-editor: Deborah Parker

Send your thoughts to
books@thomascook.com

- **Found a great bar, club, shop or must-see sight that we don't feature?**
- **Like to tip us off about any information that needs a little updating?**
- **Want to tell us what you love about this handy little guidebook and more importantly how we can make it even handier?**

Then here's your chance to tell all! Send us ideas, discoveries and recommendations today and then look out for your valuable input in the next edition of this title. As an extra 'thank you' from Thomas Cook Publishing, you'll be automatically entered into our exciting monthly prize draw.

Email to the above address (stating the book's title) or write to: CitySpots Project Editor, Thomas Cook Publishing, PO Box 227, Unit 15/16, Coningsby Road, Peterborough PE3 8SB, UK.